FORECASTING OCCUPATIONAL STRUCTURE IN A DEVELOPING ECONOMY

FORECASTING OCCUPATIONAL STRUCTURE IN A DEVELOPING ECONOMY

A Case Study of India

MONEER ALAM

CONCEPT PUBLISHING COMPANY, NEW DELHI

The Indian Council of Social Science Research financially supported the publication of this work. However, the responsibility for the contents of the book—facts, opinions, conclusions, etc.—is entirely of the author and not of the ICSSR.

First Published 1985

Published by
Naurang Rai
Concept Publishing Company
H-13, Bali Nagar
NEW DELHI-110015 (India)

Printed in India by
Ajit Singh, Printco India
Maujpur, Delhi-110053.

FOREWORD

MOST LDCs are experiencing resource constraints in their effort to accelerate the pace of their economic development. None of these countries can therefore afford a wasteful use of their productive resources—men or material. The existence of educated unemployment in India is however a clear evidence of wastage of productive manpower in this country. The unemployment of educated manpower involves wastage of resources on at least two counts. One, the cost incurred on skill formation that cannot be gainfully used amounts to wastage of scarce resources, and two, the idle skilled manpower which is in itself an important source of increased productivity remains infructuous and hence has to be treated as wastage of a resource of critical importance. Besides, unlike physical capital, idle human capital has many social and political ramifications, e.g., frustration, social tension and brain drain, etc.

In order to avoid the economic and social wastage associated with educated unemployment and to correct the imbalance between the demand for and supply of skilled manpower, a comprehensive manpower planning is necessary. This is important also because rapidly changing technology is creating demand for highly skilled and adaptable manpower. The uncontrolled effects of chance and market forces seem to be insufficient to bring about a balance between the patterns of demand for and supply of skilled manpower.

Manpower planning is however an extremely complicated affair. A major problem that confronts the planners is the forecasting of the pattern of demand for manpower. In recent years, certain techniques of manpower forecasting have been developed. In this study, Dr. Moneer Alam has used three sophisticated techniques of manpower forecasting, viz., regression analysis, the Markov probability formulation and the RAS, to investigate inter-temporal changes in the occupational structure in India. He has competently examined the predictive power of each of these three techniques both for the economy as a whole and for the manufacturing industries in the organised sector.

The results of this study would be useful for not only the research scholars working in this field but also for those engaged in the important task of manpower forecasting as a pre-requisite for manpower planning. What distinguishes this study from the previous studies is the careful use of available manpower data and a rigorous application of recent forecasting techniques. It is a scholarly work and a significant contribution to a relatively new and important area of research in India and should find favour with the informed and analytical reader.

29 August, 1984

A.M. KHUSRO
Member
Planning Commission

ACKNOWLEDGEMENTS

THIS study is a slightly modified version of my Ph. D. Thesis completed at Lucknow University (India) under the supervision of Professor H.G.P. Srivastava. I am grateful to him for his help at all stages of this work.

I was initiated into research by Professor A.M. Khusro. It was during my association with him that I became interested in issues of manpower planning. I am indebted to him for encouraging me to pursue some of the ideas developed in the study.

My thanks are also due to Professor C.H. Hanumantha Rao, then the Director, Institute of Economic Growth, for allowing me to undertake this work during my stay at the Institute. His keen interest in the work has been a source of encouragement. I owe a debt of gratitude to Professors P.C. Joshi, Ashish Bose and P.B. Desai for their advice and interest during the course of this research. Professor Ajit Dasgupta, Dr. Raghav Gaiha and the (late) Professor J.N. Sinha have provided very useful comments on various aspects of this work. Their unfailing interest in my work and meticulous comments on an earlier version of this study were invaluable. I am indeed grateful to all of them.

During the course of my research I have had useful discussions with Professor D.B. Gupta, Professor D.U. Sastry, Dr. K. Subbarao, Dr. S.A. Anwar. Dr. Sharif Mohammad, Dr. A.R. Bilgirami and Dr. D.N. Dwivedi and I would like to express my sincere appreciation of their efforts. A valuable input in this research was the programming expertise of Mr. Nazim A. Kazmi. Without his help this study would have taken a much longer period of time.

I would like to express my gratitude to the officials of the Directorate General of Employment and Training (Delhi) for providing me access to the unpublished data.

I thank the Librarian and the staff of the Institute of Economic Growth for providing me with various facilities. I am thankful to Mr. Kulbir Singh and Mr. Nand Lal for their patience and care with which they have typed the manuscript.

Finally, my thanks are also due to my parents, my wife Shahida and daughter Rabab for the patience shown and the encouragement provided to me during the course of this study. I am also indebted to my brother Professor Fasih A. Siddiqi for his role as a great sermonizer on research. His sermons kept my interest going in the present work.

August, 1984

MONEER ALAM

CONTENTS

LIST OF TABLES

LIST OF FIGURES

1

APPROACHES TO MANPOWER PLANNING

STATEMENT OF THE PROBLEM

AT the time of the formulation of the Second Five Year Plan it was anticipated that the supply of skilled manpower, viz., engineers, research and development scientists and technicians would fall short of the plan requirements. Consequently, concerted efforts were made to set up institutions for imparting the requisite skills. The plans for educational expansion were, however, made without any detailed forecasts of manpower requirements. This was partly because of the weak data base. The ambitious industrialisation programme which formed the core of the Second Five Year Plan could not achieve its targets and, as a result, manpower imbalances began to appear. These imbalances have persisted over the years. Some idea of their magnitude can be obtained from the number of engineers and other highly skilled manpower categories who are reported unemployed in recent years. The special tabulation of the 1971 Census on Degree Holders and Technical Personnel, for example, reports a very high incidence of unemployment among engineers and other categories of scientific and technical manpower. A brief description of their rates of unemployment is presented in Table 1.1.

Two points of particular significance emerge from Table 1.1. First, the highest incidence of unemployment reported is among the agricultural scientists (11.3%) followed by engineers and technologists (10.3%), while the lowest incidence is found for those holding degrees in medicine (4.3%). Secondly, as between graduates and post-graduates (including doctorates), the magnitude of unemployment is considerably larger in the former category.[1]

TABLE 1.1: **Unemployment by Education: 1971**

Education	Total number of persons	Number of persons unemployed	Rate of unemploy-ment
1. *Agricultural Science*			
(*i*) Doctorate	835	18	2.2
(*ii*) Post-graduate	7482	569	7.6
(*iii*) Graduate	29450	3699	12.6
Total	37767	4286	11.3
2. *Veterinary Science*			
(*i*) Doctorate	221	3	1.4
(*ii*) Post-graduate	1417	20	1.4
(*iii*) Graduate	8280	534	6.4
Total	9918	557	5.6
3. *Engineering and Technology*			
(*i*) Doctorate	1289	32	2.5
(*ii*) Post-graduate	11120	526	4.7
(*iii*) Graduate	89263	9965	11.2
Total	101672	10523	10.3
4. *Medicine* (*Allopathy*)			
(*i*) Doctorate	900	19	2.1
(*ii*) Post-graduate	13529	258	1.9
(*iii*) Graduate	45190	2284	5.0
Total	59619	2561	4.3

Source: Special Census of Scientific and Technical Personnel, 1971 Census (G-Series Tables).

From the trends in educated unemployment over the last two decades, it would appear that these imbalances may not correct themselves in the near future. There is thus a need for evolving an analytical framework in which educational expansion can be related to manpower requirements. The objective of this study, however, is to focus on a specific aspect of manpower forecasting, namely, the pattern of change in the occupational structure of employment over-time and its implications for educational profile of workers. This is an aspect which has received very little attention in the manpower forecasting literature for India.[2]

The procedure adopted in this study is as follows. Using the Manpower Requirement Approach an attempt is made to set up a model for forecasting the structure of employment in India. For this purpose, three different methods of manpower forecasting, namely, the traditional method, the structural method and the RAS adjustment method are chosen with a view to assessing their predictive power.[3]

The theme that we propose to develop here is that, despite its inherent regidities, the Manpower Requirement Approach can be used effectively to investigate the nature of changes in the employment profile of workers. To the extent that these changes can be correctly anticipated, a translation of these into employment levels by educational category can give some idea regarding the path of educational expansion consistent with the manpower requirements of the economy.

The scheme of this chapter is as follows. We first describe the two important approaches to educational planning, namely, the Rate of Return Approach and the Manpower Requirement Approach.[4] A synthesis of the two approaches is also discussed. Since the proposed study is based on the Manpower Requirement Approach, the concluding section brings out its relevance to the Indian situation.

ALTERNATIVE APPROACHES TO EDUCATIONAL PLANNING

There are two approaches usually employed in educational planning: (*i*) the Rate of Return Approach, and (*ii*) the Manpower Requirement Approach. We have chosen the latter. The relative merits of these approaches and the reasons for preferring the Manpower Requirement Approach are discussed below.

The rate of return approach

This approach rests on the assumption that the demand for education is determined by its profitability. This implies that so long as the private return to education exceeds its private costs (which also includes the earnings foregone due to schooling) individuals would prefer to invest in it. Similar argument would hold for the society as well. That is, until returns from investment in education accruing to society are high enough to mitigate its (total resource) cost, the society would continue to invest in it.[5]

The rates of return on resources devoted to education are often evaluated in terms of its internal rates of return.[6] The internal rate of return on investment in education is the discount rate which equates the discounted value of the future earnings anticipated from certain amount of education to the discounted value of its costs.[7]

Mathematically, the internal rate of return on investment in post-school education is a solution value of r in the following equation:

$$\sum_{t=15}^{t=60} \frac{E_t - C_t}{(1+r)^t} = 0 \qquad \ldots(1.1)$$

where r is the rate of discount, E is earnings, C is the costs of education, 15 is the school leaving age and 60 the age of retirement and t denotes time. To compute social rate of return we normally use earnings before tax and total social costs of education; while for the private rate of return we use earnings after tax and private costs of education.[8]

Solving equation (1.1) for r, and comparing the solution with relevant rate of discount, it could be concluded whether any further investment in education would be worthwhile either from a private point of view or from a social point of view. Specifically, if $r_p > \bar{r}_p$ (where r_p represents the private rate of return, and $\bar{r}_p$ is the private discount rate), it follows that investment in the course in question is worthwhile from the point of view of an individual.[9] Similarly, if the social rate of return, r_s, is larger than the given social discount rate ($\bar{r}_s$), educational investment is socially worthwhile.

These calculations require two basic sets of data: (*i*) a series of age-wise earnings classified by types and levels of education and (*ii*) data on private and social costs of education.

Assessment

While the profitability of education is an important economic explanation of private demand for education, it remains a partial explanation for several reasons. For example, it is not clear to what extent the earning differentials represent the differences in marginal productivity of labour by types and levels of education. Precisely, the equality condition between the wage rate and the value of labour's marginal product would hold under very strict conditions of perfectly competitive equilibrium. Sinha and Sawhney (1970) have shown with the Indian data that wages are determined by diverse factors; and the marginal productivity is only one of these. Dasgupta (1974) has noted that part of the higher earnings of the educated in developing countries could represent a monopoly rent on restricted entry rather than a return on education. Such restrictions may be imposed by professional bodies, by family connections and nepotism or simply by the scarcity of parents who can afford to educate their children at all.

An important problem involved in measuring the cost of education arises out of the qualitative differences in the output of educational system. If, as in India, the output is far from homogeneous the comparison of costs might not be justifiable.[10]

The measurement of earnings foregone implies that if all under-graduates were to give up their studies and seek employment their average wage would equal the average wage of a matriculate in their age-group. While this procedure might be reasonable for a marginal increase in the supply of matriculates it is likely to over-estimate the earnings forgone when a substantial increase is involved. Since not a great deal is known about the sensitivity of wages to sharp changes in the supply of different categories of educated manpower a more precise estimate is not feasible.

The estimates of returns on education are generally exclusive of its non-monetary benefits. Especially, the psychic or the spill-over benefits of education are omitted due to non-availability of data. These could, however, be the main benefits of education. The contribution that education makes to the process of social awareness (say, in regard to the family planning or new techniques in agriculture, etc.) may, for example, be extremely important for a country such as India.

An important criticism of this approach is that it is concerned totally with the demand aspects of educational planning. Hence, the supply adjustment process does not get the importance it deserves. For a complete explanation of the actual growth of the system the lags in supply must be considered alongwith the factors which determine the demand for education.[11]

The manpower requirement approach

The Manpower Requirement Approach can be represented in the form of a simple model described below.

$$L = GDP\left(\frac{GDP^s}{GDP}\right)\left(\frac{GDP_j}{GDP^s}\right)\left(\frac{L_j}{GDP_j}\right)\left(\frac{L_i}{L_j}\right)\left(\frac{L_e}{L_i}\right) \qquad \ldots(1.2)$$

where

GDP=Gross Domestic Product,

L=Labour Input,

and the scripts s, i, j, e refer to sector, occupation, industry and education, respectively; and

$$L \geqslant \sum_{s=1}^{n} L^s_{ije}$$

Equation (1.2) implies a known production function at the time of fixing the level of employment or its structure. To be more precise, it characterises the usual Leontief type fixed input-output relationship which is determined technologically—and not on economic criteria of demand with zero inter-skill or capital-labour substitution. By implication, employment (either absolute or by its components) is independent of supply; thus, if the supply of manpower in a given occupational/educational structure is changed, it will have no effect on the amount of manpower required.

While it is true that these assumptions contradict the usual price-quantity adjustment mechanism which may be important in a given situation, Ahamad and Blaug (1973) have pointed out that the structural rigidies inherent in many of the developing economies do lend some support to this argument. A rigid labour market, for example, might not produce the right type of signals either to labourers or to entrepreneurs and consequently, the wage-employment adjustment through inter-skill substitution would be hampered. Similarly, the rigidies in production technology might restrict the process of substitution between factors of production.

MANPOWER REQUIREMENT APPROACH VERSUS RATE OF RETURN APPROACH

It is now generally agreed that if the system of educational expansion is left to itself, it is highly unlikely that the actual path of educational expansion would be socially optimal. Indeed, on the contrary, the opposite may happen. This raises the question whether the process of educational expansion can be manipulated such that it leads to a stable equilibrium. It has been pointed out that this objective can be achieved by relating the educational expansion to the manpower requirements of the economy. Opinion, however, is divided on the approach to be adopted for attaining this objective.

The advocates of the Rate of Return Approach emphasise the signalling role of these calculations for educational planning purposes. The signals are, hawever, valid for marginal adjustments in the system. Also, with every adjustment the returns need to be recalculated. This is indeed a difficult requirement. Especially, the data requirements are not easily met. Layard (1972) has pointed out that a reliance on this approach with scanty evidence might be hazardous for planning the educational system.

A typical feature of the educational system is that a change in student intake influences the labour supply with a certain lag. This is especially so for certain professional courses where the lead-time required would be 5-6 years. During this period demand is unlikely to remain fixed. If demand changes drastically a reliance on the current rate of return is not appropriate as it could suggest a step in the wrong direction.

Besides, there are severe measurement problems with this formulation. To illustrate, let us take the cost of education.

As already mentioned, the cost of education includes the direct expenses and the earnings foregone of individuals. Gaiha (1977) has argued that in an economy which is characterised by severe unemployment (which renders the opportunity cost of students' time almost zero) the calculations of earnings foregone might be erroneous. Another example relates to the earning differentials. The assumption on which these calculations are based is that earnings represent the marginal value product. This assumption implies that prices represent the relative scarcities and, also that, given the prices, the marginal value product of workers can be obtained. Merrett (1966) has expressed doubts about these assumptions. Especially, in developing economies where factor markets are generally distorted partly because of the subsidies given to capital and partly because of the trade-unionism, prices seldom represent scarcities or abundance of capital and labour, respectively.[12] Moreover, often price misrepresents the real worth of a particular skill or education. For example, if the soil chemists are paid less, it would apparently imply a low productivity and hence, lower investment in this area of education. However, if it could be shown that their productivity is positively related with the size of holdings, the earnings data may yield highly erroneous conclusion.[13]

One can, therefore, argue that the Rate of Return Approach is not appropriate for planning drastic changes in the educational planning. At best, this approach can serve a signalling role for marginal adjustments. Also, this approach is too demanding in terms of data.

The Manpower Requirement Approach, on the other hand, usually relies on the assumption that both the base line skill coefficients and past trend in them are optimal. Layard (1972) points out that if the skill coefficients are falling over-time and if the rate of return has been rising at the same time to an unacceptably high level then both the base line coefficients and the trend need to be adjusted upward.

How a synthesis can raise the accuracy of the manpower forecast is shown in Fig. 1.1.

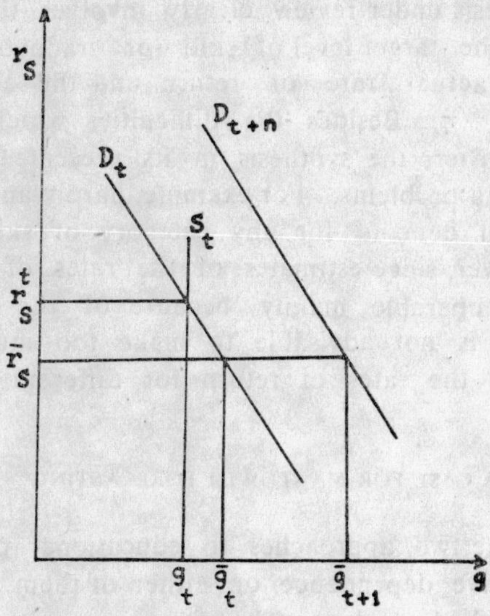

Source: Layard (1972)

Fig. 1.1

Fig. 1.1 suggests an increase in the demand for, say, graduates from g at time t to $\bar{g}$ at time $t+n$. The increase in demand can be represented as $\bar{g}_{t+n}-g_t$. This can further be broken into $\bar{g}_{t+n}-\bar{g}_t$ and $\bar{g}_t-g_t$.[14] The first component $(\bar{g}_{t+n}-\bar{g}_t)$ suggests an increase due to the growth in the demand for graduates, and the second break $(\bar{g}_t-g_t)$ is due to their current demand and supply imbalance. This imbalance is also revealed in current rate of return $(r_s{}^t)$ shown on the vertical axis in Fig. 1.1. Since the problem in manpower planning is to correct the non-optimal stock of graduate g_t to an optimal one, i.e., $\bar{g}_{t+n}$, it requires two adjustments. The first adjustment $(\bar{g}_t-g_t)=\bar{g}_t\eta\ (r_s-\bar{r}_s)/\bar{r}_s$, where η is the elasticity of demand, and the second adjustment $(\bar{g}_{t+n}-\bar{g}_t)=\bar{g}_t$ $(\dot{D}/D)t$, where $\dot{D}/D$ is the yearly optimal rate of growth and t is the number of years for which the forecast is attempted.

On the basis of this analysis Layard concludes that lower the elasticity (η) the stronger the case for forecasting.

The synthesis under review clearly involves three major calculations: the target level of skill (or graduate) requirements, their actual rate of return and the elasticity of their demand (η). Besides the difficulties which we have mentioned earlier, the synthesis in its present form poses formidable data problems. For example, hardly any estimates of elasticity of demand for any category of skill exist in India. Moreover, since estimates of the rates of return are often non-comparable mainly because of the procedural differences, it is not advisable to make too much of the differences in the rates of return for different points of time.[15]

A CASE FOR MANPOWER FORECASTING

Our view of the two approaches to educational planning is that an exclusive dependence on either of them for policy purposes may be hazardous. Therefore, we ought to regard their results only as aids to decision making in educational planning.

Since this study is mainly about forecasting the occupational structure, we will now consider whether there are any special contextual considerations which favour the use of the Manpower Requirement Approach. We will also comment on the risks which are usually associated with this approach.

Since over 65 per cent of the graduates in India are employed in the public sector and since it is easier for the government to foresee the changes in its own demands than in those of the private sector, manpower projections would perhaps turn out to be more reliable than is typically the case.

The longer the lead time the less useful the rates of return as a signalling device. Since the lead time required to develop skills in areas like medicine and engineering is higher (i.e. around 5-6 years), it is argued that Manpower Requirement Approach might be used more effectively to forecast their future requirements. The fine balancing of demand and supply which is implicit in the rate of return calculation can easily be upset over this time-span.

Especially, in developing countries discontinuities in past trends are quite significant. In an economy undergoing structural changes, technological and sectoral shifts would often necessitate fairly substantial changes in educational expansion. The decision to expand facilities for engineering education in India during the late sixties is a case in point.

Some of the criticisms of the manpower forecasting are applicable only to extreme versions of it. It is sometime argued that the Manpower Requirement Approach results in excessive specialisation. This is a mere assertion.[16]

Another criticism of this approach is that it leads to an unnecessary rigidity in educational plans. More specifically, it is argued that the usefulness of manpower forecaste depends on the validity of the output projections. If the output targets are not achieved, it would result in unnecessary rigidity in the educational plans. For this reason it is recommended that the manpower forecasting should not be a once-for-all affair but should be frequently carried out.

It could be further argued that 'the forecasts are made, not to commit the future, but simply to add another dimension to thinking about it. The fact that forecastes of this, and any other, kind are bound to be wrong to some extent, provides no logical reason for supposing that things would have been better without them. Decisions are bound to be taken on some implicit or explicit assumption about the future and a wrong forecast may well be more realistic than the assumption that would otherwise prevail' (Layard, 1972).

REFERENCES

1. Some idea about the extent of educated unemployment can also be had from recent reports of the National Sample Survey (NSS); see, for example, the NSS Report 298 based on the 32nd Round data.
2. For detailed review of the literature, see Chapter 2 of the present study.
3. For a description of these techniques, see Chapter 3 of the present study.

4. An explanation for speedier expansion of higher education can as well be drawn from the 'Hobbesian' approach in which the demand for education is treated as the rational choice of individuals; the choice being determined by interaction of such forces as social, cultural, psychological and so on. An important limitation of this approach, however, is that it fails to suggest the shifts in the pattern of educational expansion. Moreover, the wastefulness of education into Hobbesian system can only be avoided through mutual understanding between the buyers and sellers of skills, which is indeed highly impractical.
5. For definitive discussion on rates of return to education, see Schultz (1963), Becker (1964), Hansen (1963), Blaug (1967, 1970), etc. A survey of the work carried out in this area is provided in Blaug (1976).
6. Alternatively, the net present value of a project may also be considered. For the methodological details, see Dasgupta and Pearce (1972).
7. A few important limitations of the internal rate of return criterion are noted below:
   (*i*) where projects with different economic lives are being compared, the internal rate of return criterion is likely to inflate the desirability of a short life project, the internal rate of being a function both of the time periods involved and the size of capital outlay;
   (*ii*) the rate of return favours projects which bunch the benefits into the early part of their economic lives;
   (*iii*) it is quite possible to obtain more than one since the internal rate of return is the solution to a polynomial equation.
8. Note that the rate of return and the internal rate of return are used synonymously in this discussion.
9. The assumption of a uniform private discount rate ($\bar{r}_p$) implies a perfect capital market. Even though this is not realistic, a relaxation of this assumption only complicates the analysis. For a detailed discussion on this, see Layard (1972).
10. For a detailed discussion on cost and efficiency of education in India, see Pandit (1969).
11. Fields (1974) has formulated a model in which adjustment process to a given demand curve is spelt out. Gaiha (1977) has, however, shown that process of adjustment in this formulation is very lengthy and rests upon the severe assumption of fixity in the distribution of jobs. Empirically, this is a false assumption. For a realistic analysis, the implications of a growing stock of educated labour force and the increase in the number of jobs for private demand for education must be considered simultaneously.

12. For a discussion of fiscal and other measures which have distorted the relative prices of capital and labour in India, see Gupta (1977, 1983).
13. In India, because around two-third of the graduates are employed in the public sector which is believed to be over-manned, and with a salary structure which is similar to that in the private sector, there is a danger of over-estimation of marginal value product of graduates from the earnings data.
14. $\bar{g}_t - g_t$ could be negative if $\bar{r}_s > r_s$.
15. Three major rate of return exercises have been carried out for India: (*i*) Harberger (1965), (*ii*) Nallagounden (1967), and (*iii*) Blaug *et al.* (1969). For a detailed discussion on procedural differences in these studies, see Gaiha (1977).
16. For further details, see Layard (1972).

2

REVIEW OF MANPOWER FORECASTING LITERATURE

NOT much work has been done on manpower forecasting in India. The only study that uses the Indian data to forecast manpower requirements was recently carried out by Burgess, Layard and Pant (1968).[1] This is the most detailed manpower forecasting study carried out to date. The 'forecasts' of this study served as a basis for fixing the targets of educational expansion by the Education Commission.[2] It would be instructive to review the method used in this study. It will be argued here that its forecasts cannot be accepted at face value as the assumptions used in this study seem arbitrary.

BURGESS, LAYARD AND PANT ANALYSIS

The objective of the analysis by Burgess *et al.* (1968) was to provide guidelines for manpower and educational development within the framework of the perspective of economic development in India. To this end, a perspective plan for the period from 1961 to 1986 was prepared from 'Notes on a Perspective of Development in India 1960-61 to 1975-76'. It was proposed that the economy would grow during this period at an annual average rate of 6.8 per cent. The sectoral growth rates of output are presented in Table 2.1.

The method of forecasting in Burgess *et al.* (1968) is based on the Tinbergen-Bos formulation.[3] It was assumed that the number of workers with matriculation and above would grow at the same rate as net output in each sector other than services but including trade and transport. Algebraically,

$$M_t/M_o = Y_t/Y_o \qquad ...(2.1)$$

where M and Y respectively represent number of matriculates and output, and the subscripts 0 and 1 refer to initial and terminal years. Equation (2.1) may be presented as follows:

$$\frac{M_t/W_t}{M_o/W_o} = \frac{Y_t/W_t}{Y_o/W_o} \quad \ldots(2.2)$$

where W refers to workforce and rest of the symbols are

TABLE 2.1: **Sector-wise annual growth rates of output: 1961-1986**

Sector	Rate of growth (percentage)
Agriculture	3.9
Mining	9.4
Small enterprises (non-factory)	7.3
Factory establishments (with power)	10.9
Construction	10.2
Organised banking and insurance	10.7
Other commerce	6.6
Transport	8.7
Communication	9.3
Professions, liberal arts and domestic services	6.8
Government services	7.4
House property	6.1

Source: Burgess, *et al.* (1968).

defined as before. This equation is based on the postulate that the increase in the matriculate-worker ratio would be equal to the increase in average output per worker.

For the manufacturing sector, the forecasts were attempted at two levels, i.e., aggregative and disaggregative. The disaggregative forecasts were carried out after splitting the manufacturing sector into 9 sub-sectors. The estimates show considerable divergence.[4]

For the non-manufacturing sectors, especially public administration and defence, education, and other miscellaneous services including legal and business services, etc., different ratios were used. The manpower requirements of public administration and defence (which also include agricultural extension and community development) were worked out on the basis of expenditure/personnel ratios. For education and health the estimates were based on the pupil/teacher, patients/doctor and patients/nurse ratios, respectively. The minimum educational qualifications determined the requirements of educated manpower. In respect of legal and other services it was assumed that the number of matriculates and above would grow at the rate of 3 per cent per annum till 1976 and around 5 per cent per annum in subsequent years.

The total stock of educated persons was computed after multiplying the total number of workers with the reciprocal of the participation rate.

Given the actual stock of educated persons and the rate of growth over-time, a comparison is attempted between required and the likely stocks. Relying on 1961 transition proportions, Burgess *et al.* have shown that there will be a surplus of 4 million matriculates and 1.5 million graduates by the year 1986.

Confining ourselves to the methodology we find that some of the relationships are quite tenuous. Consider, for instance, the relationship between educated manpower and net output. No empirical justification is given for the assumption that the rates of growth of skilled manpower and net output are equal. This in our judgment may provide no more than a convenient first approximation.

Another difficulty with the procedure adopted by Burgess *et al.* (1968) is that a direct relationship is postulated between the rates of growth of net output and educated manpower. This may be a valid postulate if it could be shown that the distribution of jobs is fixed over the period in question. We will present some evidence (see Table 2.2) which do not lend support to the postulate made in the study under review. Specifically, the share of professionals, managerial workers, etc., in the total employment have steadily increased over time. Since there is heavy concentration of graduates and

TABLE 2.2: **Temporal variations in composition of non-manual skill categories**

(*Percentage*)

	Occupations (NCO)	Public sector			Private sector		
		1960	1966	1972	1961	1967	1973
0(—052)	Professional Workers	9.1	10.9	12.7	4.5	7.6	9.9
052	Primary and Middle School Teachers	10.4	14.4	14.1	0.6	1.2	3.0
1	Administrative, Executive Workers	5.0	5.4	5.5	1.2	1.4	1.9
2+3(—290)	Clerical and Sales Workers	15.8	14.3	15.3	7.7	8.9	9.3
4—9(+290)	Other Manual Workers	59.7	55.0	52.4	86.0	80.9	75.9
	Total: All Divisions	100.0	100.0	100.0	100.0	100.0	100.0

Source: Survey Reports of the Directorate General of Employment and Training (1960, 1961, 1966, 1967, 1972, 1973).

above in these occupations, their requirements may grow at a faster rate than those of other categories of educated manpower for a given rate of growth of output. Indeed, at the inter and intra-sectoral levels, it may be even higher. At the industrial level, there may be differences in the relationships between the rates of growth of output and educated manpower if the occupational structures are different.

These are some of the considerations which led us to concentrate on changes in the occupational structure of employment. Unless detailed forecasts of changes in the occupational structure are worked out there is very little chance of obtaining reliable manpower forecasts by educational category. Admittedly, there are some difficulties in following the procedure outlined above. These difficulties relate to the absence of a satisfactory theory linking changes in production technology and occupational profile of workers. Moreover, the coverage of the occupational data is incomplete and there is lack of uniformity in their quality.

While it is important to bear these difficulties in mind, there is no reason why attempts should not be made to utilise the data already available with a view to understanding the nature and magnitude of changes in the occupational structure of employment.

This study focuses on the occupational structure of employment in a set of manufacturing industries and on the educational implications of these changes. We have chosen to concentrate on the manufacturing sector because the occupational data are more detailed and the quality relatively good.

REFERENCES

1. Burgess, T., Layard, P.R.G. and Pant, P. (1968), *Manpower and Educational Development in India*, Oliver and Boyd, London. This was a collaborative venture of the London School of Economics, Indian Statistical Institute and the Perspective Planning Division of the Planning Commission (India).

2. For further details, see Report of the Education Commission (1964-1966).
3. For details of the Tinbergen-Bos formulation, see Appendix 2.1 of this chapter.
4. For details, refer to Table 7 in Burgess *et al.* (1968).

APPENDIX 2.1

THE TINBERGEN-CORREA-BOS MODEL

We review here the important features of the Tinbergen-Correa-Bos models.

In both the Tinbergen-Correa (1962) and Tinbergen-Bos (1964) formulations, there are two scarce labour inputs, viz., 'the total stock of people with a secondary education' and 'those with a third level of education', symbolised respectively by N^2_t and N^3_t, for the time period t. The basic relationship between these inputs and the national income or its sectoral components consists of the following equations:

$$N^2_t = V^2 v_t \quad \ldots(1)$$

$$N^2_t = (1-\lambda^2)\, N^2_{t-1} + m^2_t \quad \ldots(2)$$

$$m^2_t = n^2_{t-1} - n^3_t \quad \ldots(3)$$

$$m^3_t = n^3_{t-1} \quad \ldots(4)$$

$$N^3_t = (1-\lambda^3)\, N^3_{t-1} + m^3_t \quad \ldots(5)$$

$$N^3_t = V^3 v_t + \pi^2\, n^2_t + \pi^3\, n^3_t \quad \ldots(6)$$

N^2_t and N^3_t are the stocks of people with secondary and third levels of education at time period t. The volume of production (money) in the economy is shown by v, m^2 and m^3 represent those who have entered the labour force N^2 and N^3 within the previous six years, respectively. The number of students seeking secondary and third level education are shown by n^2 and n^3. Finally, λ and π are the adjustment coefficients to account for (*a*) the losses in stocks of N^2 and N^3, and (*b*) the output of educational sector consumed within the sector as input, respectively.

Two observations may be made here. First, the stock of labour force with secondary education is completely production oriented and, therefore, grows at a rate proportional to that of the volume of production (i.e., equation 1). From a policy viewpoint it implies that in a given time framework there can be no qualitative improvements either in N^2 or in n^2;

and factor substitutions including between N^2 and N^3 are ruled out on account of rigidies in production.[1] Second, the labour force with third level of education (i.e., N^3) consists of those involved both in production as well as in teaching of n^2 and n^3. The fraction of N^3 involved in production must grow in the same way as N^2. The values of π which account for the residual of N^3 are assumed to be 0.04 at the secondary level and 0.08 at the subsequent level of teaching.[2]

A generalization of this model was later attempted by Tinbergen and Bos (1964). Without altering the basic approach, they tried to incorporate two important modifications, namely, that the manpower requirements are related to the sectoral components of the economy rather than the entire economy and, that there might not necessarily be a proportional, but a unique, relationship between the sectoral output and its requirements for the educated manpower. These modifications are indeed important in so far as they amount to an explicit recognition of inter-sectoral differences in their requirements for the educated manpower. No such explicit distinction was made in the Tinbergen-Correa (1962) formulation. Additionally, the Tinbergen-Bos (1964) formulation considers the problem of drop-outs from the educational system.

The merits of the Tinbergen-Bos model are (*i*) its computational simplicity, and (*ii*) the minimal data requirements. The forecasts based on this model, however, are no more than a convenient first approximation. In particular, the implicit assumption of a fixed distribution of jobs over-time can introduce errors in the forecasts. Also, the assumption of zero substitution between fixed capital and skilled manpower is somewhat naive.

REFERENCES

1. For a more detailed discussion, see Sen (1966).
2. These values imply pupil-teacher ratios of 25 at the secondary level and 12.5 at higher levels of teaching.

3

TECHNIQUES FOR FORECASTING THE OCCUPATIONAL STRUCTURE OF EMPLOYMENT

THIS chapter reviews three techniques which have been used for forecasting the occupational structure of employment: (*i*) the traditional approach, (*ii*) the Markov probability formulation, and (*iii*) the R.A.S. The discussion here will focus on the assumptions underlying these techniques and their data requirements. The latter is often a decisive consideration in the choice of the technique.

THE TRADITIONAL APPROACH[1]

This approach is premised on the assumption that there is a direct and observable relationship between the occupational structure and production technology.

Let us begin with a simple production function described as below:

$$X=f(K, L) \qquad \ldots(3.1)$$

This function considers capital (K) and labour (L) as homogeneous inputs. Allowing for heterogeneity in the composition of labour the above function is modified as:

$$X=f(K, L_1, L_2, \cdots, L_n) \qquad \ldots(3.2)$$

where output is denoted by X and L_1, $L_2, \cdots, L_n$ represent different categories of skilled manpower (say, by occupation). A special form of equation (3.2) is:

$$X=min\ (K, L_1, L_2, \cdots, L_n) \qquad \ldots(3.2a)$$

Equation (3.2*a*) is a special case of equation (3.2) and implies a Leontief type of function with zero substitution between the inputs. This particular approach underlies much of the early manpower forecasting literature.[2] However, in a later version of this approach, e.g., Horowitz, Zymelman and Herrnstadt (1966), Layard and Saigal (1966), etc., the occupational structure was taken as a function of output per worker (or labour productivity). Thus, rewriting equation (3.2*a*) on the assumption of a linearly homogeneous production function, we get,

$$X/L = f(K/L, L_1/L, L_2/L, \cdots, L_n/L) \quad \ldots(3.3)$$

Layard and Saigal (1966) point out that none of the preceding equations necessarily implies a unique relationship between output and total employment or its skill component, as the input-proportions associated with different levels of output are determined by their relative market prices. Provided an additional assumption is introduced that for every X/L, there is one and only one set of L_i/L's and K/L, a demand equation for each occupation can be expressed as a function of X/L. The form chosen for estimation by Layard and Saigal (1966) is given below:

$$\text{Log}\,(L_i/L) = \alpha + \beta \log\,(X/L) \quad \ldots(3.4)$$

This equation was estimated at the sectoral level with the help of cross-country data.

There are some obvious difficulties with this approach:

(*i*) The assumptions of linearly homogeneous production function for different sectors may be arbitrary.

(*ii*) The estimation procedure is merely a convenient one. The simplification introduced in deriving the demand equation may result in an estimation bias. Specifically, the representation of technology in terms of labour productivity is not at all persuasive.

(*iii*) A more serious difficulty stems from the separate treatment of each occupational category. This overlooks the complementarities and substitution possibilities between different skills.[3]

An extension of this approach was carried out by the Organisation for European Cooperation and Development (OECD).[4] This study develops a much broader framework within which alternative specification of technology is combined with important economic indicators of development to explain cross-country differences in occupational proportions. This is designed to highlight that the influence of technology is conditioned by a host of institutional and environmental factors.

Algebraically,

$$L_i/L=f(n) \quad \cdots (3.5)$$

where n represents a set of technological, economic and non-monetary indicators (the notation is borrowed from the OECD study). Some of the important variables used in the OECD study include output per worker, a non-monetary indicator of development, say, energy consumption per worker, etc. However, the results presented in this study are vitiated by multicollinearity among some of the explanatory variables. Moreover, the coefficients of non-monetary variables in some exercises were not significant. The study, however, shows that inclusion of additional variables (i.e., variables other than X/L) raises the explanatory power of the equation.

A common feature of empirical studies based on this approach is that they posit an instantaneous adjustment between skill structure and technological changes. Given the delays and the costs of recruitment, it is unlikely that a complete adjustment between the occupational structure and technology would take place instantaneously. Allied to this is the question whether a direct relationship between the occupational structure and technology is legitimate. If the adjustment is through inter-occupational mobility the relationship becomes an indirect one and accordingly the specification should be modified.

THE MARKOV PROBABILITY FORMULATION

This formulation is distinguishable from the production function approach in two respects:

(*i*) Changes in occupation-wise employment are viewed as interdependent, and

(*ii*) Changes in the occupational profile are caused by inter-occupational mobility.

A simple version of the Markov probability formulation was recently employed by ILO (1971). This is the version we have experimented with.

The evolution of the occupational structure is viewed as a stochastic process in which inter-occupational movements are governed by a first-order Markov process.

The transition probabilities are computed with the help of a linear programming model. An algebraic description of the model is given below:

Definitional equation:

$$L_{t+1} = L_t . P + U_{t+1}$$

Objective function:

$$\sum_{t=1}^{T-1} (U'_{t+1} + U''_{t+1}) . I \quad \ldots \text{Min}$$

Constraints:

$$\sum_{J=1}^{n} p_{ij} = 1, \ \forall i$$

$$p_{ij} \geqslant 0, \ \forall i, \ \forall j$$

$$\left.\begin{matrix} u'_{t+1} \geqslant 0, \\ u''_{t+1} \geqslant 0, \end{matrix}\right\} \forall t$$

where

L_t = a row vector of employment by occupation expressed as a proportion of total employment $(1 \times n)$ in year t;

L_{t+1} = a row vector of employment by occupation expressed as a proportion of total employment $(1 \times n)$ in year $t+1$;

P = a matrix of transition probabilities $(n \times n)$;

U_{t+1} = a row vector of residuals $(1 \times n)$ between the observed L_{t+1} and $L_t . P$. For computational purposes U_{t+1} is expressed as the difference between U'_{t+1} and U''_{t+1} which is to be minimised[5]; and

I = represents an identity vector.

This model minimises the sum of absolute deviations subject to the constraints that the elements of P are non-negative and the row sums are unity (i.e., $\sum_{j=1}^{n} p_{ij}=1$).

For projection purposes, given an initial occupational vector, the transition matrix is first raised to an appropriate power, and then post multiplying the occupational vector by the transition matrix the occupational proportions are obtained. It is suggested that a mobility index, M, can also be obtained from the transition matrix.

$$M=\frac{\text{sum of the probabilities off the diagonal}}{\text{sum of the probabilities on the diagonal}}$$

or

$$M=\frac{n}{t_r}-1,$$

where n is the number of occupational categories and t_r is the sum of probabilities along the principal diagonal. For a given country, the higher the index M the greater the degree of mobility.

The advocates of this approach [ILO (1971), Sabolo (1971)] claim that this approach is intuitively more appealing and less demanding in terms of data requirements than the production function approach. These claims are supported by forecasts which approximate closely the observed occupational structure. Two observations are necessary here:

First, in this method, given an initial equilibrium, the adjustment process is assumed to be completed within a year. Considering that the inter-occupational movements may require formal training, job experience, etc., and that these requirements may differ by types of skills or occupations, a partial adjustment process seems to be more plausible. The second problem concerns the adequacy of the data to estimate inter-occupational mobility. Whichever method of estimation is used, it is doubtful that reliable estimates of inter-occupational mobility can be computed from a time-series of skill proportions alone.[6] These must be supplemented by data on occupation-wise earnings differentials, age distribution of workers, period of training for acquiring new skills, etc.

THE RAS ADJUSTMENT METHOD

This relatively simple technique for adjusting the elements of a matrix from given row and column totals for a subsequent year has been extensively used in recent years.[7] The evolution of a matrix over-time is governed by row and column effects interacting multiplicatively. An important feature of this adjustment is that its data requirements are minimal, viz., an initial matrix, and row and column totals for the year of adjustment. Algebraically,

$$\hat{A} \quad \hat{r} \quad \hat{s}$$

$$\hat{A}_{t+k} = \hat{r} A_t \hat{s} \qquad \text{...(2.6)}$$

where A_t and $\hat{A}_{t+k}$ are base and projected matrices, and $\hat{r}$ and $\hat{s}$ are the diagonal matrices of row and column multipliers.

Now, suppose A_t is known, and also the row and column totals of A_{t+k}, so that

$$A_{t+k}\, i = U_{t+k} \qquad \text{...(2.7)}$$

$$A'_{t+k}\, i = V_{t+k} \qquad \text{...(2.8)}$$

where i is a column vector and U_{t+k} and V_{t+k} are the column vectors of row and column sums, respectively. Bacharach (1970) has shown that provided there is at least one matrix satisfying (2.7) and (2.8), then there is one and only one, A_{t+k}, which satisfies all the equations. The row and column multipliers (i.e. $\hat{r}$ and $\hat{s}$, respectively) are estimated in an iterative procedure. Some important features of the adjustment are:

(*i*) Zero elements in the base year matrix remain zero in the adjusted matrix.

(*ii*) Computationally, the adjustment is not too demanding as the convergence is usually quick.

(*iii*) If the base year matrix is non-negative then the adjusted matrix will also be non-negative.

Detailed experiments using alternative formulations with British occupational data were carried out by a team of experts at Warwick University. Their results were generally favourable to the RAS adjustment (see Bosworth *et al.*, 1974). A recent application of this technique to Indian occupational data also produced favourable results (Gaiha, 1977). Encouraged by these results we have carried out detailed exercises using Indian manufacturing data.

Two questions may be asked: (*i*) is the bi-proportional hypothesis a plausible one, and (*ii*) can an economic meaning be given to the row and column effects? While the biproportional hypothesis seems to approximate observed changes in occupation-industry matrices, there is a real danger that this adjustment might not correctly approximate changes in cells with relatively smaller values.[8] As far as the interpretation of the row and column effects as substitution and fabrication effects is concerned, it should be noted that this interpretation rests on the presumption that the wage-quantity mechanism of hiring skills across the industries is identical. This may or may not be true.

Adherence to a strict proportionality rule as a representation of temporal movements of skill coefficients may not be wholly justifiable if the coefficients are subject to errors in measurement and other random disturbances. A modified RAS adjustment which admits of random disturbances around biproportional movements seems to be intuitively more appealing. There are, however. difficulties in using this procedure. First, it requires occupation-industry matrices for different points of time. For instance, Johansen's formulation (1968) requires at least two complete matrices. The second difficulty arises from insufficient knowledge about deviations from biproportionality. In the absence of such knowledge, alternative assumptions about the disturbances leading to different formulation may turn out to be equally plausible.

REFERENCES

1. The production function approach is sometimes referred to as the traditional approach [see, for example, Sabolo (1971)].
2. See, for instance, Parnes (1962).
3. Dougherty (1972) has shown that the utilisation of different skills is partly conditioned by their relative supplies. Even though the model

is not rigorously worked out and the data are of uneven quality, Dougherty's results ought not to be ignored.

4. Organisation for European Cooperation and Development (OECD), Paris (1970), Occupational and Educational Structures of the Labour Force and Levels of Economic Development, Possibilities and Limitations of an International Comparison Approach.
5. For detailed derivation of this, see Lee *et al.* (1965).
6. Note that Sabolo (1971) relaxes the assumption of stationary transition probabilities and develops a more flexible formulation in which transition probabilities are related to the supply of educated manpower and the consumption demand.
7. An early application of this method was attempted by Deming and Stephan in demography (reference cited in Lecomber (1969). In the Cambridge Growth Project (1963), this method was used to obtain an input-output matrix for 1960. Since then this method has been extensively applied in various fields including foreign trade, manpower, etc.
8. For a more detailed discussion on this, see Chapter 7 of the present study.

Note: Sign (∧) indicates estimated value.

4

DATA ON OCCUPATION BY INDUSTRY

THIS chapter reviews the major sources of occupational data for India. Specifically, the focus is on the classifications used, and the coverage of the occupational statistics.

This chapter is organised as follows: First, the occupational data sources are described. This is followed by a discussion of the usability of the data for forecasting purposes.

DATA SOURCES

In India, two important sources which provide industry-wise occupational data are the decennial population censuses and the reports of the surveys conducted by the Directorate General of Employment and Training (D.G.E. & T.). A brief account of both these sources is presented below.

Decennial population censuses

A break-up of employment by major sectors of the economy was first attempted in the 1961 census. Unlike other data sources an important advantage lies with the censal data in its coverage. However, this advantage is often offset by inter-censal changes in definitions.

The 1961 census classifies workers according to the National Classification of Occupation (NCO), 1958. The classification was, however, modified in the next census, as it was based on NCO, 1968. Despite the fact that both the classifications were developed by the D.G.E. & T., a strict matching between them, especially at the 2 and 3 digit levels, poses formidable problems.

Moreover, the definition of 'worker' used in the 1971 census was different from that used in the 1961 census. As a result, the 1971 census reports a considerable decline in the working force participation rate (see Shrinivasan and Raj, 1977). Despite a resurvey conducted by the Office of the Registrar General (i.e., paper 1 of 1974) and a host of other independent attempts to account for the gap in working force participation rate during this period, the problem remained more or less unresolved.[1] Finally, the census data on the occupational profile of workers are available only for two points of time, i.e., 1961 and 1971.[2]

Surveys of the D.G.E. & T.

Another source of occupational data which is available on a regular basis since 1961 is the surveys of the public and private sectors carried out by the D.G.E. & T. in alternate years. The primary data are obtained by the Directorate from public establishments in the public sector (excluding defence and other installations of public importance) and non-agricultural establishments in the private sector[3] employing 25 or more workers, on a statutory basis. Establishments employing 10-24 workers in the private sector are, however, covered on a voluntary basis. Smaller establishments which are indeed substantial both in terms of number and total employment are, thus, excluded.

The occupational data are presented in terms of the NCO, 1958, which consists of 11 occupational divisions (one digit level), 75 occupational groups (two digit level), 331 occupational families (three digit level) and a further sub-division of these families into 1990 occupations (five digit level).[4] Using the Standard Industrial Classification (1960) prepared by the Directorate on the lines suggested by the UN's adopted International Standard Industrial Classification (1958), these occupations are cross-tabulated by industries. The industrial classification follows the Standard Industrial Classification (SIC) which consists of 9 industrial divisions (one digit level), 45 major groups (two digit level) and 343 minor group (three digit level).

We have decided to rely on the D.G.E. & T. data because of the fact that (*a*) the data are fairly comprehensive, and (*b*) these are available at short interval (i.e., every alternate year for public and private sectors).

Since we have used unpublished data which include vacancies by occupation in each industry, we were faced with the choice of including them in constructing a base year occupation-industry matrix. Opinions differ on this issue. The logic of their inclusion is that the existing employment and vacancies put together represent the employers' optimal labour requirement. This argument implies that vacancies are accurately reflected by employers' estimates of additional numbers they would employ at the current wage rate, provided the potential persons were available in the job market. A contrary view is that, since the current level of production is achieved by the existing employment, it represents the minimum requirements. Jolly and Colclough (1972) argue that the optimum requirements lie somewhere between these two extremes. They recommend that the mid-value can be taken as a convenient approximation. The closeness of the approximation, however, depends on the shapes of the supply and demand curves. We decided against this approximation on the following grounds:

(*a*) the data on vacancies cover barely 10 per cent of the establishments; and
(*b*) in most cases, the vacancies bear no or very little relation to actual requirements at the prevailing wage rate.

LIMITATIONS OF THE D.G.E. & T. DATA

We now comment on some important limitations of the D.G.E. & T. data. The two limitations which have serious implications for our analysis are (*a*) incomplete coverage, and (*b*) incorrect reporting of occupations.

As already pointed out, the D.G.E. & T. provides occupation-industry data on a survey basis for public and private sectors in every alternate year. The coverage of this survey varies sharply between the two sectors because of lack of uniformity in response rates of public and private establishments. Besides, in each sector the response rate varies over time. Sector-wise non-response rates for different points of time and the resulting underestimation of employment are presented in Table 4.1.

We can see from Table 4.1 that the variation in terms of both establishments and employment covered is considerably large in both the sectors. Underestimation is particularly acute in manufacturing establishments. Surprisingly, the response rate of manufacturing establishments in the public sector is relatively low. This is a serious limitation of the data and, for our statistical analysis, adjustments had to be made largely on the basis of information supplied to us by the D.G.E. & T.

An adjustment was applied to the employment data. The adjustment factor based on information given in Table 4.1 is derived as follows:

$$E_A = \frac{E_s}{E_T} E_{ij} \qquad \ldots(4.1)$$

where

E_A = adjusted employment

E_s = estimated employment[5]

E_T = total employment of all the observed industries and

E_{ij} = share of ith occupation in total employment of industry j.

Admittedly, any adjustment is bound to be somewhat arbitrary and our adjustment is no exception. However, in the absence of any further information this is the only adjustment which could be made.

Another data limitation is the misreporting of occupations by the responding establishments. Even though all the establishments were supplied with the specimen lists of occupation for assisting them in describing the occupations in clear and unambiguous terms, some used a general terminology such as Director, Supervisor, Foreman, Mistry, Engineer, etc., without indicating the exact occupational family. In such cases, they were occupationally classified, wherever possible, on the basis of educational qualifications shown against such posts. In other cases, they were classified on the

TABLE 4.1: **Response rates of establishments in public and private sectors**

	Private sector			Public sector		
	1963	1967	1971	1964	1966	1972
1. Total Number of Establishments	28,924	34,924	36,065	43,620	52,423	68,624
2. Total Estimated Employments (in lakhs)	53.49	57.06	59.13	80.10	94.90	115.40
3. Number of Establishments Submitting Returns	25,317	28,433	28,968	37,164	44,618	57,000
4. Employment in Responding Establishments (in lakhs)	44.53	38.78	45.81	63.34	67.38	80.20
5. Percentage of Responding Establishments	87.72	81.41	80.32	85.20	85.11	83.06
6. Percentage of Employment Reported	83.25	67.96	77.47	79.08	71.00	69.50
7. Estimated Employment in Manufacturing Sector (2+3) (in lakhs)	—	32.92	37.61	—	6.88	9.21
8. Employment in Responding Manufacturing Establishments (in lakhs)	—	20.31	27.40	—	3.44	4.93
9. Percentage to Estimated Employment in Manufacturing Sector	—	61.70	72.85	—	50.00	53.53

Note: '—' stands for not available.

Source: Reports of the D.G.E. & T. on Occupational Pattern in India (1963, 1964, 1966, 1967, 1971, 1972).

basis of available ancillary information, e.g., local knowledge of establishment and the duties of the posts involved. Some bias may have been introduced in favour of administrative posts as against professional ones.

CLASSIFICATION AND AGGREGATION IN OCCUPATION-INDUSTRY MATRICES

Two areas of aggregation are: (*i*) the industrial, and (*ii*) the occupational classifications. Two features of occupation-industry matrices are:

(*a*) highly skewed distrbution of certain skills, and
(*b*) the presence of a large number of null cells.

A fine break-up of occupations and industries is usually preferred. Since many of the skills in the manufacturing sector are industry—specific or insignificant—due to their negligible share in the total employment,[6] the usefulness of a detailed occupational break-up cannot be taken for granted. On the other hand, however, analysis based at higher levels of aggregation might suffer from insensitiveness in the skill coefficients or from the heterogeneity bias or both.

To get an idea of the loss of information in alternative aggregation schemes we have used some concepts of information theory. Based on the results of the following exercises a choice of occupational classification is made.

APPLICATION OF JOINT INFORMATION ENTROPIES TO INDIAN OCCUPATION-INDUSTRY DATA

The objective of this exercise is to assess the loss of information associated with different schemes of occupational aggregation obtained for a cross-section of manufacturing industries for the years 1963-64 and 1971-72. Considering that this is one of the few applications of entropy in this area, a brief description of entropy is necessary.[7]

Concept and estimation of entropies

Consider an arbitrary event, E, whose probability of occurrence is P. If the event is almost certain to occur (i.e., suppose $P(E)=0.98$), practically no information is received as the occurrence of E was certain. On the other hand, if $P(E)$ is reduced to .01, an occurrence of event E will give a great deal of information. Hence an inverse relationship between the probability P and the quantity of information or information entropy $h(P)$ is postulated. The inverse relationship is expressed as:

$$h(p)=\log \frac{1}{p}=-\log p \quad \ldots(4.2)$$

This function ranges from ∞ (i.e. infinite information if the $P=0$) to 0 (i.e., zero information if $P=1$). To determine the unit of information it is customary to use logarithm of base 2, which implies a unit value of information [i.e., $h(1/2)=1$] when the probability of occurrence and non-occurrence of event E is 0.5 each. The logic of using the function given in Eq. 4.2 stems from its property of additivity. The minus sign ensures that $h(P)$ will always be positive. A graphic representation of the inverse relationship between information entropy $h(p)$ and the probability P is shown in Fig. 4.1.

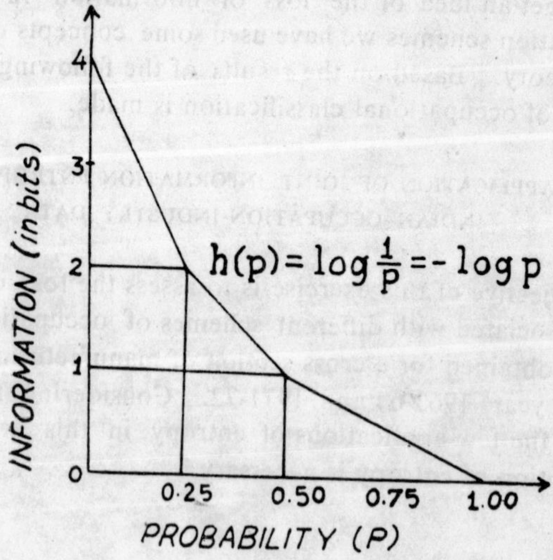

Fig. 4.1

So far we were concerned with single event. Now, suppose there is a set of n mutually exclusive events, $E_1, E_2, E_3, \ldots, E_n$ with probabilities $p_1, p_2, p_3, \ldots, p_n$. Since the E_s are mutually independent, $\Sigma p_n = 1$. As the event which is due to occur is unknown *a priori*, the information (h) of the set of n events is defined to be a weighted average of log p_i. Algebraically,

$$-p_1 \log p_1 - p_2 \log p_2 - p_3 \log p_3 \ldots - p_n \log p_n$$

$$= -\sum_{i=1}^{n} p_i \log p_i \qquad \ldots(4.3)$$

The value of $-\sum_{i=1}^{n} p_i \log p_i$ is the entropy which measures the average information (or average uncertainty) associated with a set of n mutually exclusive events. This value is maximum when $p_1 = p_2 = p_3 = \ldots p_n = \frac{1}{n}$ and $H_{max} = \text{Log}(n)$.[8] The lowest value is always equal to zero. Thus, the entropy, H, ranges from zero to Log (n).

To estimate the joint entropies of our occupation-industry matrix, L_{ij}, we have employed bivariate information theory.[9] The subscripts i and j of this matrix represent the proportionate distribution of employment in ith occupation and jth industry such that the row and column totals give occupation and industry-wise total employment, respectively. Symbolically,

$$L_i = \sum_j L_{ij} \;\forall i \qquad \ldots(4.4)$$

and

$$L_j = \sum_i L_{ij} \;\forall j \qquad \ldots(4.5)$$

Also, the aggregate employment L is,

$$L = \sum_i L_i = \sum_j L_j = \sum_i \sum_j L_{ij} \qquad \ldots(4.6)$$

The intersection of L_i and L_j is shown below:

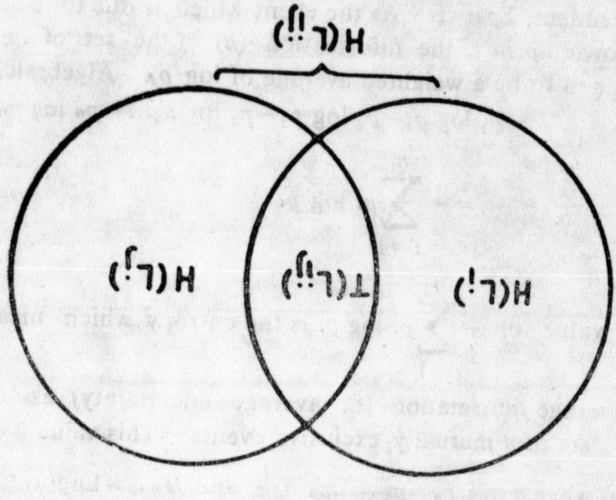

Fig. 4.2

The circles $H(L_i)$ and $H(L_j)$, as pointed out before, characterise the proportionate distribution of aggregate employment, L, by occupation and industry, respectively. The joint entropy $H(L_{ij})$ relates to the pattern of occupational classification summed over all industries. It also represents the total information existing in the matrix in question. To what extent the L_is and L_js are interlinked is shown by the common portion $T(L_{ij})$. The $T(L_{ij})$ is essentially non-negative and can assume a zero value, if and only if, the L_is and L_js are stochastically independent.

Converting them into a bivariate probability distribution and following the definition given in (4.3), we write,

$$H(L_i) = -\sum_i p_i \log p_i \qquad \ldots(4.7)$$

where

$$p_i = \frac{L_i}{L} \quad \forall_i$$

$$H(L_j)=-\sum_{j} p_j \log p_j \qquad \ldots(4.8)$$

where

$$p_j=\frac{L_j}{L} \quad \forall_j$$

$$H(L_{ij})=-\sum_{i}\sum_{j} p_{ij} \log p_{ij} \qquad \ldots(4.9)$$

where

$$p_{ij}=\frac{L_{ij}}{L} \quad \forall_i,\ \forall_j$$

$$T(L_{ij})=\left(-\sum_{i} p_i \log p_i\right)+\left(-\sum_{j} p_j \log p_j\right)$$
$$-\left(-\sum_{i}\sum_{j} p_{ij} \log p_{ij}\right) \qquad \ldots(4.10)$$

or $T(L_{ij})$ may also be expressed as:

$$T(L_{ij})=H(L_i)+H(L_j)-H(L_{ij}).$$

Application of entropies to alternative schemes of occupational disaggregation

Using the D.G.E. & T. data, we compute the information entropies of five different employment profiles drawn for a set of 81 manufacturing industries of public and private sectors for the years 1963-64 and 1971-72.[10] The consolidated occupation-industry matrices are prepared after adjusting for the underestimation of employment in public and private sectors.[11]

Alternative aggregation schemes are shown in Table 4.2.[12] For convenience we have focused on professional skills. Since these skills are highly diverse[13] both functionally as well as in terms of their educational requirements, considerable care is required in developing alternative aggregation schemes.

The results

Table 4.3 summarises the results for 1963-64. The results obtained for 1971-72 are given in Table 4.4. We note from these tables that a shift from group A to group B sharply reduces the information content. The values of $H(L_i)$ which represents the information content of a specific employment profile decline from 2.283 to 2.269 in 1963-64 and from 2.141 to 2.126 in 1971-72. The corresponding values of $H(L_{ij})$ and

TABLE 4.2: **Group-wise list of occupations**

Sl. No.	Group A	Group B	Group C	Group D	Group E
1	00	00-01	00-01-02	00-01-02	Div. 0
2	01	02	03-08	03-0X	Div. 1
3	02-08	03-08	09-0X	Div. 1	Div. 2
4	09-0X	09-0X	Div. 1	Div. 2	Div. 3
5	Div. 1	Div. 1	Div. 2	Div. 3	Div. 4
6	Div. 2	Div. 2	Div. 3	Div. 4	Div. 4
7	Div. 3	Div. 3	Div. 4	Div. 5	Div. 6
8	Div. 4	Div. 4	Div. 5	Div. 6	Div. 7
9	Div. 5	Div. 5	Div. 6	Div. 7	Div. 8
10	Div. 6	Div. 6	Div. 7	Div. 8	Div. 9
11	Div. 7	Div. 7	Div. 8	Div. 9	
12	Div. 8	Div. 8	Div. 9		
13	Div. 9	Div. 9			

Note: Group A denotes 13 occupations and 81 industries;
Group B denotes 13 occupations (the scheme of occupational aggregations is different from that of Group A) and 81 industries;
Group C denotes 12 occupations and 81 industries;
Group D denotes 11 occupations and 81 industries; and
Group E denotes 10 occupations and 81 industries.

$T(L_{ij})$ also decline. While both the groups (i.e., A and B) consist of 13 occupations, the latter group combines Architects, Engineers, etc., (NCO 00) together with the Chemists, Physicists, and other related Physical Scientists (NCO 01). The inverse relationship between the level of occupational aggregation and information entropies [i.e. $H(L_i)$] is confirmed by the results obtained for the subsequent three groups, i.e., groups C, D and E.[14] These groups represent successively higher levels of aggregation.

TABLE 4.3: **Information entropies of occupation-industry matrix: 1963-64 (No. of industries 81)**

Occupational Groups	No. of Occupations	$H(L_i)$	$H(L_j)$	$H(L_{ij})$	$T(L_{ij})$	$T(L_{ij})/H(L_i)$ (%)	$T(L_{ij})/H(L_j)$ (%)
A	13	2.283 (.617)	4.859 (.766)	6.780 (.675)	.363	15.900	7.470
B	13	2.269 (.613)	4.859 (.766)	6.771 (.674)	.358	15.778	7.368
C	12	2.266 (.632)	4.859 (.766)	6.769 (.682)	.357	15.754	7.347
D	11	2.243 (.648)	4.859 (.766)	6.747 (.688)	.355	15.827	7.306
E	10	2.187 (.658)	4.859 (.766)	6.699 (.693)	.348	15.911	7.162

Note: Values in parentheses give the coefficients of adjusted entropies, i.e., H/H_{max}.

TABLE 4.4: **Information entropies of occupation-industry matrix: 1971-72 (No. of industries 81)**

Occupational Groups	No. of Occupations	$H(L_i)$	$H(L_j)$	$H(L_{ij})$	$T(L_{ij})$	$T(L_{ij})/H(L_i)$ (%)	$T(L_{ij})/H(L_j)$ (%)
A	13	2.141 (.578)	5.047 (.796)	6.807 (.678)	.382	17.842	7.569
B	13	2.126 (.574)	5.047 (.796)	6.797 (.677)	.377	17.733	7.470
C	12	2.124 (.592)	5.047 (.796)	6.795 (.685)	.376	17.702	7.450
D	11	2.105 (.608)	5.047 (.796)	6.778 (.692)	.374	17.767	7.410
E	10	2.060 (.620)	5.047 (.796)	6.738 (.697)	.369	17.913	7.311

Note: Values in parentheses give the coefficients of adjusted entropies, i.e., H/H_{max}.

The more interesting results relate to the coefficients of adjusted entropies.[15] Tables 4.3 and 4.4 present these coefficients. It can be seen from these tables that the adjusted values of entropies are not inversely related to levels of aggregation. Indeed, the relationship is a positive one. Unlike the unadjusted entropies, the adjusted entropies tend to rise as we move to higher levels of occupational aggregation To illustrate, the results for 1963-64 in Table 4.3 show that adjusted $H(L_i)$ varies between 0.617 for group A to 0.658 for group E. Of the two, the former is more disaggregated (see Table 4.2). For 1971-72 the corresponding range is from 0.578 to 0.620, respectively. A similar pattern is also suggested by the coefficients of adjusted $H(L_{ij})$ for both points of time. One possible explanation is that there is a large number of null cells in more disaggregative classifications. H may therefore diminish while H_{max} increases and, hence, the adjusted value is smaller for disaggregated classifications.

A high value of adjusted $H(L_j)$ implies that inter-industry differences in absolute employment are relatively low.[16] Moreover, we notice that these differences have reduced over time. For example, while the value of adjusted $H(L_j)$ was 0.766 for 1963-64, it was 0.796 for 1971-72. This might have been brought about by relatively high increases in employment in some relatively small industries.

As expected, the values of $T(L_{ij})$ are not very high. This suggests that the information content of our occupation-industry matrices is moderate. This may be partly on account of a large number of null cells in the occupation-industry matrix. That the level of occupational aggregation of non-professional skills is very high may be yet another reason for the low values of $T(L_{ij})$.

We note from Table 4.3 that the loss of information in moving from group A to group B is not negligible. While for group A, the $T(L_{ij})$ for 1963-64 is 0.363, for group B it is only 0.358. From B to D, the loss of information is negligible. But between D and E the loss of information is again not negligible. This pattern is reproduced in 1971-72 (see Table 4.4).

Normalised values of $T(L_{ij})$ in terms of occupational and industrial entropies, i.e. $T(L_{ij})/H(L_i)$ and $T(L_{ij})/H(L_j)$ in

Tables 4.3 and 4.4 present an interesting contrast. While the normalised value of group E in terms of occupational entropy is highest, group A turns out to be the best in terms of the industrial entropy.

Out of the alternative occupation-industry matrices considered, it is evident that in terms of the information content the occupation-industry matrix represented in group A is clearly superior.[17] Hence in much of the subsequent empirical work, we have employed this occupation-industry matrix.

REFERENC

1. For an attempt to reconcile the difference, see Sinha (1972).
2. The data for 1981 was not available at the time when this study was completed.
3. Plantations are included in D.G.E. & T. reports.
4. The D.G.E. & T. has for the first time in 1974 introduced the code structure of NCO, 1968. Before that occupational classification followed the pattern given in NCO, 1958. We were unable to use the 1974 data because of lack of comparability.
5. Both aggregate and sector-wise estimates of total employment are furnished by the D.G.E. & T. in its reports. These estimates are derived by the Directorate from the information which it collects under the Employment Marketing Information (EMI) Programme. After making the necessary adjustments in respect of establishments which did not submit returns these figures are obtained. An industry-wise break-up of non-response rates is not presented.
6. Some of the industry specific skills include Architects, Engineers, Chemists, Physicists, Biologists, Agronomists, etc The production workers distributed skewedly are Farmers, Hunters, Loggers, Mining and Quarrymen and so on. The skills which are negligible in terms of their share in employment are Jurists. Artists, Writers, Directors, Managers Financial Institutions, Insurance and Real State Salesmen, etc.
7. The only other application of entropy to occupational classification is contained in OECD (1971).
8. For a formal derivation, see Theil (1972).
9. For a detailed discussion on bivariate and multivariate information theory, see Theil (1967, 1972).
10. A list of the industries is given in Appendix 4.1 of this chapter.
11. For a discussion on the limitations of combining the corresponding skills of public and private sector manufacturing establishments, see the next chapter.

12. For a description of the occupations corresponding to the codes. see Appendix 4.2 of this chapter.
13. The diversity of skills among professional workers can be judged from the fact that this category lumps together development scientists, engineers, economists, doctors, jurists, creative artists, writers etc.
14. For further details, see Tables 4.3 and 4.4.
15. Adjusted entropies are the normalised value of H. This value is the ratio H/H_{max}. The maximum entropy is equal to log n (where n denotes the number of categories). An advantage of using this measure is that it facilitates the comparison of entropies associated with different number of categories.
16. The coefficient of adjusted $H(L_j)$ remains constant for all the groups in question because we do not aggregate industries.
17. Note here that if we were concerned only with the occupational classification group A classification will not be chosen on grounds of information content. However, since the focus of this study is on occupation-industry matrices, it is the value of $T(L_{ij})$ which is crucial.

APPENDIX 4.1

LIST OF INDUSTRIES

Sl. No.	SIC Codes	
1	200	Production of rice, atta, flour, etc., by milling, dehusking of crops and foodgrains
2	201	Production of sugar and syrup in mills.
3	202	Production of indigenous sugar and gur, etc.
4	203	Production of fruit products, e.g., jam, jelly, sauce, etc.
5	205	Production of bread, biscuit and cake, etc.
6	206	Production of butter, ghee, cheese and other dairy products
7	207	Production of edible fats and oils (o.t. Vanaspati)
8	208	Production of hydrogenated oils (Vanaspati)
9	209	Production of other food products, e.g., sweetmeat and condiments, chira, chocolate, etc.
10	210—13	Production of distilled spirits, wines, country or indigenous liquors, etc.
11	214+19	Production of aerated and mineral water and other beverages
12	217	Processing of tea in factories
13	220—26	Manufacture of tobacco products
14	230	Cotton ginning, cleaning, pressing and baling
15	231—36 (—33)	Cotton spinning in mills, powerlooms and handlooms and manufacture of khadi textile in handlooms
16	239	Manufacture of cotton, cordage, rope and twine
17	240	Jute pressing and baling
18	241	Jute spinning and weaving
19	252—55	Wool spinning and weaving in mills, powerlooms and handlooms, etc.
20	260—64 (—61)	Spinning, weaving and dyeing of silk textiles in mills, powerlooms and handlooms
21	270	Manufacture of carpet and other similar textile products
22	271	Manufacture of hosiery and other knitted fabrics and garments
23	272	Embroidery and making of crepe lace and fringes
24	273	Manufacture of textile garments including rain coats and head gears

Sl. No.	SIC Codes	
25	275+79	Manufacture of waterproof textile products, e.g., oil cloth, tarpulin, etc., and manufacture of other textile products (n.e.c.)
26	277	Manufacture of coir and coir products
27	278	Manufacture of umbrellas
28	280	Sawing and planing of wood
29	281	Manufacture of wooden furniture and fixtures
30	290–91	Manufacture of pulp and paper in mills and handmade
31	292	Manufacture of paper products as paper bags, boxes, moulded pulp goods from paper and pulp
32	302–03	All types of printings and bindings
33	310	Currying, tanning and finishing of hides and skins and preparation of finished leather
34	311	Manufacture of shoes and other leather footwear
35	313	Manufacture of leather products (excluding shoes and wearing apparel)
36	320	Manufacture of tyres and tubes
37	321	Manufacture of rubber footwear
38	322—23	Manufacture of rubber goods for industrial purposes and other rubber products from synthetic or natural rubber
39	324	Production of petroleum and its products in refineries
40	325—26	Production of coaltar and coal and their products
41	330	Manufacture of basic industrial chemicals, e.g., acid, alkalis, etc.
42	331	Manufacture of dyes, paints and colours, etc.
43	332	Manufacture of fertilizers
44	333	Manufacture of ammunition and explosives
45	334	Manufacture of matches
46	335	Manufacture of medicines and pharmaceutical preparations and cosmetics.
47	336	Manufacture of soap and other washing compounds
48	337+39	Manufacture of turpentine, synthetic and plastic products and other chemicals or their products (n.e.c.)
49	340	Manufacture of structural clay products
50	341	Manufacture of cement and cement products
51	343	Manufacture of structural stone goods
52	347	Manufacture of asbestos products
53	348	Manufacture of mica products
54	351	Manufacture of chinaware and crockery
55	354	Manufacture of glass apparatus
56	357	Manufacture of glass and glass products (excluding glass apparatus and optical and photographic lenses, etc.)

Sl. No.	SIC Codes	
57	359	Manufacture of other non-metallic mineral products
58	360	Manufacture of iron and steel
59	361	Manufacture including smelting, refining of non-ferrous metals and alloys
60	363	Manufacture of structural steel products
61	368	Enamelling, galvanising, plating and polishing of metal products
62	369	Manufacture of sundry hardwares and sundry ferrous engineering products
63	370	Manufacture and assembling of machinery (o.t. electrical) except textile machinery
64	371	Manufacture and assembling of prime mover and boilers (o.t. diesel engines, tractors or road rollers)
65	372	Manufacture of machine tools
66	373	Manufacture of textile machinery and accessories
67	374	Manufacture of heavy electrical machinery
68	375	Manufacture of electric lamps and fans
69	376	Manufacture of insulated wires and cables
70	377	Manufacture of all kinds of battery
71	380	Manufacture, assembly and repairing of locomotives
72	381	Manufacture of wagon, coaches and tramways, etc.
73	382	Manufacture and assembling of motor vehicles (except engines)
74	384	Repairing and servicing of motor vehicles
75	385+89	Manufacture of bicycles and tricycles and accessories and other transport equipment
76	386	Building and repairing of water transport equipment
77	387	Manufacture and repair of air transport equipment including planes and engines
78	391	Manufacture of scientific, medical and surgical instruments
79	392	Assembling and repairing of watches and clocks
80	395	Manufacture of stationery articles such as pencils, fountain pen, etc.
81	396	Manufacture of sports goods

APPENDIX 4.2

DESCRIPTION OF OCCUPATIONS (NCO, 1958)

Sl. No.	NCO Codes	Occupations
1	00	Architects, engineers and surveyors
2	01	Chemists, physicists, geologists and other physical scientists
3	02	Biologists, veterinarians, agronomists and related scientists
4	03-08	Physicians, surgeons, nurses, pharmacists, teachers, jurists, social scientists, artists, writers and related workers
5	09-0X	Draughtsmen, science and engineering technicians (n.e.c.) and other professional, technical and related workers
6	Div. 0	Professional, technical and related workers
7	Div. 1	Administrative, executive and managerial workers
8	Div. 2	Clerical and related workers
9	Div. 3	Sales workers
10	Div. 4	Farmers, fishermen, hunters, loggers and related workers
11	Div. 5	Miners, quarrymen and related workers
12	Div. 6	Workers in transport and communication occupation
13	Div. 7	Craftsmen, production process workers and labourers (n.e.c.)
14	Div. 8	Craftsmen, production process workers and labourers (n.e.c.)
15	Div. 9	Sports and recreation workers

5

APPLICATION OF THE TRADITIONAL APPROACH TO THE INDIAN DATA: MANUFACTURING SECTOR

THREE alternative approaches to forecasting the occupational structure were discussed in Chapter 3. We now take up their applications. In this chapter, we report the results based on an application of the traditional approach in which the occupational structure is determined by technological and other production characteristics. In our application of this approach, we have followed largely the specifications used in OECD study (1970). A major advantage of this formulation is that alternative technological specifications can be tried without explicitly specifying a production function.

Our objective in this chapter is, therefore, to relate the occupational proportions to a set of technological and other related factors. In order to check for the robustness of the results, three cross-sections for 1963-64, 1966-67 and 1971-72 are analysed.

The scheme of this chapter is as follows. First, a few important assumptions of the model are described. This is followed by a discussion of the specification of the relationships to be estimated. In the next section, we describe the nature and limitation of the data used in our statistical analysis. The final section is devoted to discussion of the statistical results.

THE ASSUMPTIONS[1]

Our model assumes: (*i*) that there is a direct relationship between the occupational structure and the production technology, and (*ii*) that there is no substitution between different skills after a technique is chosen.

Keeping these assumptions in mind, we have made an attempt here to understand how the occupational structure has evolved with the help of this approach.

THE MODEL

The strategy followed here is that we first consider the complete sample of manufacturing industries. This is followed by sub-groups of industries, each sub-group comprising industries which appear to be technique-wise more homogeneous.

First formulation[2]

This formulation is based on the following estimating equation:

$$\text{Log } (L_{ij}/\sum_i L_{ij}) = \alpha + \beta_1 \text{ Log } (T_j) + \beta_2 \text{ Log } (E_j/I_j) + \beta_3 \text{ Log } (X_j/F_{nj}) + e_j \qquad \ldots(5.1)$$

where

L=total employment;

T=factor intensity variable;

E/I=share of expenditure on electricity, fuel, etc., in total input expenditure;

X/F_n=average value added per unit of firm in the observed industry;

(i=1, 2,..., m) number of occupations;

(j=1, 2,..., n) number of industries (or observations); $m \neq n$ and for each i, k equations are estimated (the number of equations varies).

T_j in equation (5.1) serves as a representation of technological characteristics. Three alternative specifications of T_j are used, namely, (*a*) fixed capital/value added ratios (K_j/X_j), (*b*) total employment/value added ratios (L_j/X_j) and (*c*) fixed capital/total employment ratios (K_j/X_j). Equation (5.1) is estimated separately for each of the three cross-sections for the entire sample of manufacturing industries.

Second formulation

So far we have been concerned with the entire sample of industries. The regression equation given in (5.1) implies that the observed industries lie on the same production surface.

To test for the assumption implied in equation (5.1), we have employed an alternative formulation using slope and intercept dummies. A list of these variables is given below.

We have classified the observed group of industries into five sub-groups,[3] namely, (*i*) agriculture based industries, (*ii*) mining and metals based industries, (*iii*) chemical based industries, (*iv*) engineering industries, and (*v*) miscellaneous industries. For a total of five industrial sub-groups, 4 intercept and 20 slope dummies are used.[4] These dummies are as under:

	Agriculture based industries	Mining and metals based industries	Chemicals based industries	Engineering industries
Intercept Dummies (δ)	D_1	D_2	D_3	D_4
Slope Dummies (γ)				
K/X	D_5	D_6	D_7	D_8
(T_j) L/X	D_9	D_{10}	D_{11}	D_{12}
K/L	D_{13}	D_{14}	D_{15}	D_{16}
E/I	D_{17}	D_{18}	D_{19}	D_{20}
X/F_n	D_{21}	D_{22}	D_{23}	D_{24}

With the inclusion of dummies, equation (5.1) becomes,

$$\text{Log}\,(L_{ij}/\sum_i L_{ij})=\alpha+\delta\,(D_1)+\beta_1\,\text{Log}\,(K_j/X_j)$$

$$+\beta_2\,\text{Log}\,E_j/I_j)$$

$$+\beta_3\,\text{Log}\,(X_j/F_{nj})+e_j \qquad \ldots(5.2)$$

$$D_1 \begin{cases} =1, \text{ if the industries belong to the agro-based group;} \\ =0, \text{ if they belong to other sub-groups.} \end{cases}$$

$$\text{Log}\,(L_{ij}/\sum_i L_{ij})=\alpha+\beta_1\,\text{Log}(K_j/X_j)+\gamma_5(D_5.K_j/X_j)$$
$$+\beta_2\,\text{Log}(E_j/I_j)+\gamma_{17}(D_{17}.E_j/I_j)$$
$$+\beta_3\,\text{Log}(X_j/F_{nj})+\gamma_{21}(D_{21}.X_j/F_{nj})$$
$$+e_j \qquad \ldots(5.3)$$

D_5, D_{17}, D_{21} $\begin{cases} =1, \text{ if the industries belong to the agro-based group;} \\ =0, \text{ if they belong to other sub-groups.} \end{cases}$

$$\text{Log}\,(L_{ij}/\sum_i L_{ij})=\alpha+\delta(D_1)+\beta_1\,\text{Log}(K_j/X_j)+\gamma_5(D_5.K_j/X_j)$$
$$+\beta_2\,\text{Log}(E_j/I_j)+\gamma_{17}(D_{17}.E_j/I_j)$$
$$+\beta_3\,\text{Log}(X_j/F_{nj})+\gamma_{21}(D_{21}.X_j/F_{nj})$$
$$+e_j \qquad \ldots(5.4)$$

D_1, D_5, D_{17}, D_{21} $\begin{cases} =1, \text{ if the industries belong to the agro-based group;} \\ =0, \text{ if they belong to other sub-groups.} \end{cases}$

The δ and γ in the last three equations represent the coefficients of the intercept and the slope dummies, respectively. If these coefficients turn out to be statistically significant, the inference is that the occupational pattern in the observed sub-group of industries is different from that in the remaining sub-groups.

Choice of explanatory variables

The choice of explanatory variables was constrained by the lack of detailed production data for the observed set of industries. In all, five variables are chosen. These variables are defined below.

The labour/output ratios are used as the technological variable. Since a given amount of labour per unit of output is associated with varying quantities of capital, we have also used the fixed capital-output and the fixed capital-labour ratios as proxies for the production technology.

Another variable, representing the share of expenditure on power, fuel, etc., in the total input expenditure (E/I), is used as a measure of automation in production. Average output per unit of firm (X/F_n) may be regarded as a scale indicator.

Some other relevant variables which could not be included for paucity of data are, say, the organizational structure, managerial attitudes, share of expenditure on research and development, location of the establishments, etc.

THE DATA

The exercise is based on a sample of 81 manufacturing industries, cross-classified by their employment profiles, for the years 1963-64, 1966-67[5] and 1971-72 at all India level. Two sets of data are used. The industry-wise occupational data are obtained from the unpublished records of the D.G.E. & T. Since the production characteristics of these industries are not furnished by the D.G.E. & T., we have supplemented the D.G.E. & T. data with the Annual Survey of Industries (hereafter referred to as ASI). This, however, posed some problems.

Two problems may be mentioned. One is the difference in their coverage of establishments. For example, the D.G.E. & T. covers all the public establishments (excluding installations of public importance) in the public sector and non-agricultural establishments (but including plantations) in the private sector, employing 25 or more workers. The establishments covered in the ASI, on the other hand, are those which employ 50 or more workers with the aid of power and 100 or more workers without the aid of power.[6]

Secondly, the ASI collects and reports annual data and does not distinguish between public and private sector establishments. As the D.G.E. & T. provides skill profiles for these sectors separately, we were left with no choice except to combine them so that the two data sets become comparable.

There are, however, some risks in aggregating the corresponding skills of these two groups of industries. An important problem, for example, is the difference in their occupational composition. It is observed, for instance, that the proportion of professional workers in the public sector establishments is relatively larger.[7] This is also true for some other categories of non-manual workers.[8] Similarly, the two groups of industries may also differ in terms of their scale of operation or choice of technology. It would, therefore, be interesting to do this exercise separately for public and private sectors. This is, however, not possible with the data available to us.

Some of the definitions used in the ASI are given below.

Fixed capital
It comprises the land, buildings including those under construction, improvement to land and other construction; plant, machinery and tools (including un-installed); transport equipment and other fixed assets such as furniture, fixtures, etc. It includes fixed assets under construction, installation and assets at head office allocable to factor.

Number of persons employed
The average number of persons employed by each factory under various heads such as workers, other than workers, etc. is computed by taking the total attendance of persons in all the shifts on all working days and dividing it by the number of days worked. These averages are aggregated for all factories in the State or industry, as the case may be, and the aggregate is taken as the number of persons employed in the State or industry, respectively. It includes persons attending and on leave with pay, such as sick leave, casual leave or paid vacation and also those engaged in welfare activities.

Fuel, electricity consumed
This excludes any fuel or material manufactured within the factory and consumed in it, e.g., electrical energy generated and consumed within the factory. The coal used in generating the energy is, however, included since it is brought into the factory from outside. Materials consumed for repair and maintenance are included. The value of materials, etc. consumed is the cost at the factory. It includes the purchase price, transport charges and other incidental costs.

Material input

It is the gross value of materials, fuels, etc. consumed, work done by other concerns, products reported for sale last year but used for further manufacture, incidental expenditure on purchase of materials, etc., non-industrial services purchased, depreciation and purchase value of goods sold in the same condition as purchased. Non-industrial services purchased include amounts paid on account of adult fee, accounts and bank charges, legal expenses, insurance charges, local rates and factory licences, etc.

Value added by manufacture

This represents that part of the value of the products which is created in the factory and is computed by deducting from the gross ex-factory value of output, the gross value of input.

In many cases, the industrial classification used in the ASI differs from that of the D.G.E. & T. An attempt is, therefore, made to match those industries with the help of manuals of industrial classification prepared by the Central Statistical Organisation (CSO) and D.G.E. & T. In some cases, the correspondence between the two classifications is an approximate one.[9] Especially, the two classifications are not strictly comparable for such industries as the manufacture of basic industrial chemicals (SIC 330), manufacture and assembling of machinery (other than electrical) except textile machinery (SIC 370), etc.

THE FINDINGS

The results are presented for 13 occupations, over three points of time, viz., 1963-64, 1966-67 and 1971-72. A two-tailed '*t*' test is applied to the regression coefficients.[10]

Some comments on the inter-relationships between the explanatory variables are necessary. The correlation matrices for the three cross-sections are presented in Tables 5.1-A, B and C. These tables suggest a high positive linear relationship between K/X and K/L ratios. We also notice from these results that the K/L and L/X as well as the L/X and X/F_n ratios are negatively correlated with high r_s. While these relationships appear to be plausible—as they have the expected signs—there is a risk of multicollinearity. To circumvent this difficulty we have decided to retain only those variables which not only explain the variability in the occupational proportions to a significant extent but also hold a meaningful relationship with correct sign.

TABLE 5.1-A: **Correlation matrix: 1963-64**

(No. of observations 81)

	K/X	L/X	K/L	E/I	X/F_n
K/X	1.000	—.144	.771	.514	.126
L/X		1.000	—.678	—.053	—.676
K/L			1.000	.391	.590
E/I				1.000	.163
X/F_n					1.000

TABLE 5.1-B: **Correlation matrix: 1966 67**

(No. of observations 77)

K/X	1.000	.008	.624	.434	.163
L/X		1.000	—.623	—.068	—.545
K/L			1.000	.361	.526
E/I				1.000	.190
X/F_n					1.000

TABLE 5.1-C: **Correlation matrix: 1971-72**

(No. of observations 81)

K/X	1.000	.045	.524	.247	—.120
L/X		1.000	—.720	—.066	—.819
K/L			1.000	.345	.560
E/I				1.000	.178
X/F_n					1.000

Finally, a few words about the dummy variables. As already pointed out, a straightforward application of regression analysis treating each industry as a unit of observation would imply that all industries lie on the same production function, which on *a priori* grounds, might not be acceptable. The severity of this assumption, however, could be somewhat reduced in two ways. One is to allow for differences in intercept, and the other is to allow for differences in response to the dependent variable to a unit change in an explanatory variable (or variables) between industries (i.e., differences in slope). In our analysis, this is achieved by introducing intercept and slope dummies. With the inclusion of these dummies, not only some of the non-quantifiable differences between industries are captured but also the bias in the coefficients of the explanatory variables, which could otherwise exist, might be reduced.

DISCUSSION OF OCCUPATION-WISE RESULTS

We first consider the results for some of the minor occupational categories within the group of professional workers.[11] Our findings for the broad occupation divisions will be discussed subsequently. The occupation-wise results—obtained for the three cross-sections—are presented in Tables 5.2 to 5.14. These tables are further arranged in three parts (i.e., A, B and C) to indicate the years to which the results relate.

(00) **Architects, engineers, surveyors, etc.**

Two important points can be noted from the results shown in Tables 5.2-A, B and C. First, the scale of production (X/F_n) and the automation in production (E/I) turn out to be the crucial determinants of these skills. Second, the coefficients of these variables are numerically smaller for later years.

The significance of X/F_n at the 1 per cent level of significance for the first two cross-sections and at the 5 per cent level for the third and E/I at the 1 per cent level for the first cross-section and 5 per cent for the subsequent two with positive signs indicate a complementarity between skills in question and the scale and degree of automation in production. A decline in their coefficients, however, implies that the extent of these complementarities is reduced over time. A reduction in the coefficient of X/F_n suggests that the assumption

TABLE 5.2-A: **Multiple regression analysis: 1963-64**

Dependent Variable: Log $(L_{ij}/\sum_i L_{ij})$

(00) *Architects, engineers and surveyors, etc.* (*No. of observations 81*)

		Log (K/X)	Log (L/K)	Log (K/L)	Log (E/I)	Log (X/F_n)	Intercept Dummy (δ)	Slope Dummies (γ)	R^2	$\bar{R}^2$	F
All industries											
1.	—5.675	1.327			.809	1.410			.260	.231	9.0
	(—3.655)	(1.730)†			(1.377)	(3.590)**					
2.	—2.053		—2.907		1.523				.245	.225	12.6
	(—2.271)		(—3.847)**		(3.028)**						
3.	—4.635			1.288	.890	.849			.275	.247	9.7
	(—3.117)			(2.158)*	(1.648)†	(1.781)†					
Engineering industries							D_4				
4.	—2.124		—2.700		1.541		1.174		.288	.260	10.4
	(—2.403)		(—3.625)**		(3.136)**		(2.161)*				

Values in brackets give '*t*' values

* Significant at 5 per cent level of significance

** Significant at 1 per cent level of significance

† Significant at 10 per cent level of significance

TABLE 5.2-B: **Multiple regression analysis: 1966-67**
Dependent Variable: Log $(L_{ij}/\sum_{i} L_{ij})$

(00) *Architects, engineers and surveyors, etc.* (*No. of observations 77*)

		Log (K/X)	Log (L/X)	Log (K/L)	Log (E/I)	Log (X/F_n)	Intercept Dummy (δ)	Slope Dummies (γ)			R^2	$\bar{R}^2$	F
All industries													
1.	—4.642 (—4.251)	1.770 (4.041)**			.029 (.072)	.794 (2.885)**					.316	.288	11.2
2.	−1.221 (—1.619)		—.604 (—1.014)		.901 (2.176)*						.076	.051	3.0
3.	—3.787 (—3.213)			.397 (1.014)	.570 (1.351)	.720 (2.070)*					.175	.141	5.2
Agriculture based industries													
							D_1	D_5	D_{17}	D_{21}			
4.	—4.800 (—4.518)	.417 (.610)			−.222 (−.563)	.888 (3.134)**	—.710 (—2.212)*	2.459 (2.809)**	.052 (.042)	—.686 (—.495)	.424	.365	7.3

Mining and metals based industries										
					D_6	D_{18}	D_{22}			
5.	—4.849	1.488	—.177	.860	1.126	.017	—.217	.364	.309	6.7
	(—4.383)	(3.301)**	(—.434)	(2.959)**	(2.227)*	(.028)	(—.369)			
Chemicals based industries										
					D_7	D_{19}	D_{23}			
6.	—5.111	2.137	—.262	.901	—.985	—.292	—1.057	.362	.308	6.6
	(—4.514)	(4.038)**	(—.608)	(3.072)**	(—2.221)*	(—.868)	(—1.010)			

Values in brackets give '*t*' values
*Significant at 5 per cent level of significance
**Significant at 1 per cent level of significance

TABLE 5.2-C: **Multiple regression analysis: 1971-72**

Dependent Variable: $\text{Log}\,(L_{ij}/\sum_i L_{ij})$

(00) *Architects. engineers, surveyors, etc.* (*No. of observations 81*)

		Log (K/X)	(Log (L/X)	Log (K/L)	Log (E/I)	Log (X/F_n)	Intercept Dummy (δ)	Slope Dummies (γ)	R^2	$\bar{R}^2$	F
	All industries										
1.	—3.081	.512			.459	.628			.157	.124	4.8
	(—3.592)	(1.598)			(1.482)	(2.628)*					
2.			—.859		.676				.124	.101	5.5
			(—2.256)*		(2.275)*						
3.	—2.741			.716	.395	.203			.178	.146	5.6
	(—3.409)			(2.419)*	(1.283)	(.876)					
	Agriculture based industries										
							D_1				
4.	—2.804	.506			.229	.408	—.550		.207	.165	5.0
	(—3.313)	(1.617)			(.716)	(2.002)*	(—2.199)*				
	Engineering industries										
							D_4				
5.	—1.754		—.759		.693		.608		.170	.138	5.3
	(—3.254)		(—2.019)*		(2.380)*		(2.083)*				

Values in brackets give '*t*' values

*Significant at 5 per cent level of significance

of constant returns to scale may not be consistent with the evidence for different points of time.[12]

As regards the *L/X* ratios, we find that in contrast to the results for 1963-64 and 1971-72, this variable ceases to be statistically significant in 1966-67. The sign of the coefficient, however, does not change.

With the exception of engineering industries, the results of the dummy variables are mostly uneven. A notable point in this connection, however, is—which is true for the engineering industries as well—that the intercept dummies systematically perform better than the slope dummies.

(01) **Chemists, physicists, geologists, etc.**

We note from Tables 5.3-A, B and C that the variables representing automation in production (*E/I*) and labour productivity (*L/X*) perform better in explaining inter-industry variation in the share of skills associated with this occupational group. Both the variables are statistically significant at the 1 per cent level for 1963-64 with positive and negative signs, respectively. It is interesting to note that the coefficients of these variables turn out to be significant at the 5 per cent level in the subsequent years (i.e., 1966-67 and 1971-72). Moreover, the coefficient of *L/X* ceases to be statistically significant in 1971-72.

Another variable which appears to have explanatory power is the capital-labour (*K/L*) ratio. We find from Tables 5.3-A, B and C that the coefficient of this variable is statistically significant with a positive sign for all the three cross-sections. Unlike *E/I* or *L/X*, the level of its significance improved from 5 per cent in 1963-64 and 1966-67 to 1 per cent in 1971-72. Interestingly, we observe that when *K/L* is used with *E/I*, the latter ceases to be significant. Presumably, this is because of the multicollinearity.

In addition to the variation in the demand for this occupational group associated with technical and scale characteristics, the slope and intercept dummies also account for some variation (see Tables 5.3-A, B and C).

TABLE 5.3-A: **Multiple regression analysis: 1963-64**

Dependent Variable: Log $(L_{ij}/\sum_i L_{ij})$

(01) *Chemists, physicists, geologists, etc.* (*No. of observations 81*)

		Log (K/X)	Log (L/X)	Log (K/L)	Log (E/l)	Log (X/F_n)	Intercept Dummy (δ)	Slope Dummies (γ)			R^2	$\bar{R}^2$	F
All industries													
1.	—8.468	.881			1.507	2.026					.227	.197	7.5
	(−3.691)	(.778)			(1.736)†	(3.490)**							
2.	—4.404		−4.962		2.104						.295	.277	16.3
	(−3.490)		(—4.702)**		(3.000)**								
3.	—7.552			1.773	1.254	1.228					.260	.232	9.2
	(−3.479)			(2.033)*	(1.590)	(1.765)+							
Agriculture based industries													
							D_1	D_5	D_{17}	D_{21}			
4.	−8.383	1.192			1.601	1.822	.829	—.315	—1.115	.665	.274	.204	3.9
	(—3.518)	(.714)			(1.805)†	(2.871)**	(1.111)	(—.135)	(—.407)	(2.004)*			
Mining and metals based industries													
							D_2	D_6	D_{18}	D_{22}			
5.	—8.824	.705			1.573	1.737	1.454	−3.600	—2.316	1.015	.335	.271	5.3
	(—3.856)	(.612)			(1.810)†	(2.936)**	(1.543)	(−2.707)**	(—1.981)*	(1.034)			

TABLE 5.4-C: **Multiple regression analysis: 1971-72**

Dependent Variable: Log $(L_{ij}/\sum_i L_{ij})$

(09-0X) *Draughtsmen, science and engineering technicians and other professional workers* (*No. of observations 81*)

		Log (K/X)	Log (L/X)	Log (K/L)	Log (E/I)	Log (X/F_n)	Intercept Dummy (δ)	Slope Dummies (γ)			R^2	$\bar{R}^2$	F
All industries													
1.	−4.214	.693			.391	.688					.112	.078	3.2
	(−3.377)	(1.485)			(.368)	(2.353)*							
2.	−2.446		−1.102		681						.081	.058	3.4
	(−3.059)		(−1.993)*		(1.579)								
Engineering industries													
								D_8	D_{20}	D_{24}			
3.	−3.397	.613			1.060	.494		−.615	−.659	−.135	.179	.113	2.7
	(−2.592)	(1.335)			(1.997)*	(1.483)		(−2.129)*	(−1.450)	(−2.186)*			

Values in brackets give '*t*' values

*Significant at 5 per cent level of significance

TABLE 5.5-A: **Multiple regression analysis: 1963-64**

Dependent Variable: Log $(L_{ij}/\sum_i L_{ij})$

(0) Professional, technical and related workers *(No. of observations 81)*

		Log (K/X)	Log (L/X)	Log (K/L)	Log (E/I)	Log (X/F_n)	Intercept Dummy (δ)	Slope Dummies (γ)		R^2	$\bar{R}^2$	F
All industries												
1.	—2.759 (—8.324)	.521 (3.182)**			.087 (6.94)	.416 (4.958)**				.389	.365	16.3
2.	—1.572 (—7.672)		—.799 (—4.662)**		.351 (3.075)**					.296	.278	16.4
3.	—2.362 (—7.490)			.459 (3.622)**	.134 (1.758)†	.217 (2.146)*				.409	.386	17.8
Agriculture based industries												
							D_1	D_9	D_{17}			
4.	—1.582 (—7.861)		—.386 (—3.157)**		.225 (1.850)†		— 714 (—1.852)†	.201 (1.540)	.639 (2.047)*	.364	.322	8.6
Engineering industries												
							D_4					
5.	—2.598 (—8.023)	.487 (3.090)**			.115 (.957)	.356 (4.270)**	.319 (2.728)**			.443	.414	15.1

							D_4						
6.	—1.597		—.726		.357		.414				.393	.370	16.6
	(—8.337)		(—4.495)**		(3.351)**		(3.515)**						
							D_4						
7.	—2.204			.462	.151	.149	.352				.475	.448	17.2
	(—7.267)			(3.848)**	(1.387)	(1.516)	(3.102)**						
							D_4	D_8	D_{20}	D_{24}			
8.	—2.453	.470			.191	.294	.549	—.091	—.314	.088	.498	.450	10.4
	(—7.425)	(3.024)**			(1.448)	(3.299)**	(2.079)*	(—1.239)	(—2.729)**	(.241)			
								D_8	D_{20}	D_{24}			
9.	—2.382	.499			.179	.280		—.061	—.280	—.562	.469	.426	10.9
	(—7.092)	(3.153)**			(1.330)	(3.090)**		(—.826)	(—2.460)*	(—2.872)**			

Values in brackets give '*t*' values
*Significant at 5 per cent level of significance
**Significant at 1 per cent level of significance
†Significant at 10 per cent level of significance

TABLE 5.5-B: **Multiple regression analysis: 1966-67**

Dependent Variable: Log $(L_{ij}/\sum_i L_{ij})$

(0) *Professional, technical and related workers* (*No. of observations 77*)

		Log (K/X)	Log (L/X)	Log (K/L)	Log (E/I)	Log (X/F_n)	Intercept Dummy (δ)	Slope Dummies (γ)		R^2	$\bar{R}^2$	F
All industries												
1.	—2.280	.545			.023	.246				.409	.385	16.8
	(—8.194)	(4.886)**			(.228)	(3.508)**						
2.	—1.336		—.348		.285					.145	.122	6.3
	(—6.717)		(—2.214)*		(2.607)**							
3.	—1.994			.408	.093	.096				.380	.354	14.9
	(—7.115)			(4.392)**	(.933)	(1.164)						
Agriculture based industries												
							D_1					
4.	—2.197	.506			—.042	.213	—.178			.448	.417	14.6
	(—8.039)	(4.595)**			(—.404)	(3.042)**	(—2.248)*					
								D_9	D_{17}			
5.	—1.426		—.280		.154			—.066	.787	.288	.249	7.2
	(—7.654)		(—1.891)†		(1.418)			(—2.221)*	(2.881)**			

Mining and metals based industries													
								D_6	D_{18}	D_{22}			
6.	−2.324	.475			−.044	.251		.313	−.047	.004	.466	.421	10.2
	(−8.367)	(4.193)**			(−.431)	(3.441)**		(2.463)*	(−.314)	(.030)			
Chemicals based industries													
								D_{15}	D_{19}	D_{23}			
7.	−1.927			.269	.136	.112		.008	.107	.605	.430	.380	8.8
	(−6.702)			(2.334)*	(1.293)	(1.371)		(2.152)*	(1.065)	(2.423)*			
Engineering industries													
							D_4						
8.	−1.885			.387	.120	.063	.258						
	(−6.957)			(4.338)**	(1.249)	(.787)	(2.779)**						
							D_4	D_{12}	D_{20}				
9.	−1.396		−.095		.233		.433	−.218	−.227		.309	.260	6.3
	(−7.492)		(−.526)		(2.150)*		(3.963)**	(−1.315)	(−2.236)*				

Values in brackets give '*t*' values
*Significant at 5 per cent level of significance
**Significant at 1 per cent level of significance
†Significant at 10 per cent level of significance

TABLE 5.5-C: **Multiple regression analysis: 1971-72**

Dependent Variable: Log $(L_{ij}/\sum_i L_{ij})$

(0) Professional, technical and related workers *(No. of observations 81)*

	Log (K/X)	Log (L/X)	Log (K/L)	Log (E/I)	Log (X/F_n)	Intercept Dummy (δ)	Slope Dummies (γ)	R^2	$\bar{R}^2$	F
All industries										
1.	—2.093	.299			.205	.283		.306	.279	11.3
	(—7.193)	(2.750)**			(1.956)†	(4.149)**				
2.	—1.439		—.546		.324			.277	.259	15.0
	(—7.691)		(—4.217)**		(3.203)**					
3.	—1.912			.546	.134	.047		.440	.418	20.1
	(—7.695)			(5.260)**	(1.408)	(.653)				
Agriculture based industries										
							D_1			
4.	—1.984	.297			.150	.236	—.216	.362	.329	10.8
	(—6.987)	(2.825)**			(1.072)	(3.447)**	(2.579)*			
							D_1			
5.	—1.405		—.449		.238		—.187	.318	.291	12.1
	(—7.655)		(—3.346)**		(2.237)*		(—2.140)*			
							D_1			
6.	—1.827			.511	.073	.023	—.164	.471	.443	16.9
	(—7.420)			(5.027)**	(.754)	(.318)	(—2.125)*			

Mining and metals based industries													
							D_2	D_7	D_{19}	D_{23}			
7.	—2.033	.271			.146	.274	—.141	.335	—.096	—.001	.392	.334	6.7
	(—6.644)	(2.570)*			(1.313)	(3.697)**	(—1.207)	(2.867)**	(—.354)	(—.318)			
Engineering industries													
							D_4						
8.	—1.979	.289			.225	.238	.288				.379	.346	11.6
	(—7.071)	(2.782)**			(2.248)*	(3.572)**	(2.977)**						
							D_4						
9.	—1.444		—.493		.332		.316				.368	.343	14.9
	(—8.200)		(—4.019)**		(3.493)**		(3.319)**						
							D_4						
10.	—1.804			.540	(1.520)	.003	.296				.516	.490	20.3
	(—7.690)			(5.611)**	(1.703)†	(.037)	(3.464)**						
								D_8	D_{20}	D_{24}			
11.	—1.911	.205			216	.220		—.052	.146	1.177	.405	.356	8.7
	(—7.633)	(1.853)†			(2.079)*	(3.063)**		(—.516)	(1.674)†	(2.818)**			

Values in brackets give '*t*' values

*Significant at 5 per cent level of significance

**Significent at 1 per cent level of significance

†Significant at 10 per cent level of significance

The capital/output (K/X) and the capital-labour (K/L) ratios are used alternatively (with E/I and X/F_n) to examine the nature of the relationship between proportions of professional workers and the capital used per unit of output and labour across the sample of industries. Tables 5.5-A, B and C show that both the variables are positively related to the share of skills associated with this occupation division. The coefficients of these variables are significant at the 1 per cent level for all the three cross-sections. It is, therefore, reasonable to infer that the demand for professional and technical workers would tend to rise with an increase in capital intensity of production.

This is further confirmed by the significance of the coefficient attached to the L/X and the E/I ratios. These coefficients are statistically significant at the 1 per cent level for the three years in question (the only exception is the coefficient of L/X ratios which is significant at the 5 per cent level in 1966-67). The negative sign associated with the L/X, which is the reciprocal of the average labour productivity, implies a higher labour productivity with the rise in share of these skills.

The results in Tables 5.5-A, B and C also indicate a strong positive relationship between these skills and the scale of production (X/F_n). This is borne out from the fact that the coefficient of X/F_n is statistically significant for all the cross-sections at the 1 per cent level.

The 't' test—used to examine whether or not the coefficients are equal to unity—reveals that invariably the coefficients are below unity.

The fact that the dummies turn out to be significant for all groups of industries as against only for engineering industries (and to some extent, agriculture based industries) in 1963-64 implies that technological and scale characteristics are not adequately captured by the explanatory variables in later years.

(Div. 1) Administrative, executive and managerial workers

None of the relationships tried on our data for 1963-64

TABLE 5.6-B: **Multiple regression analysis: 1966-67**
Dependent Variable: Log $(L_{ij}/\sum_i L_{ij})$

(1) *Administrative, executive and managerial workers* (*No. of observations 77*)

		Log (K/X)	Log (L/X)	Log (K/L)	Log (E/I)	Log (X/F_n)	Intercept Dummy (δ)	Slope Dummies (γ)			R^2	$\bar{R}^2$	F
All industries													
1.	−2.054			.161	—.164	—.077					.091	.053	2.4
	(−9.231)			(2.272)*	(—2.062)*	(−1.172)							
Mining and metals based industries													
							D_2	D_{14}	D_{18}	D_{22}			
2.	—2.260			.120	—.312	—.082	.683	.490	—.201	—.042	.207	.126	2.6
	(—9.398)			(1.609)	(−3.326)**	(−1.268)	(2.892)**	(2.838)**	(—1.617)	(—.356)			
Engineering industries													
							D_4	D_{16}	D_{20}	D_{24}			
3.	−1.944			.204	— 189	—.153	—.360	.758	—.067	—.395	.220	.141	2.8
	(—8.428)			(2.658)**	(−2 411)*	(−1.954)†	(—1.426)	(2.560)*	(—.962)	(—1.071)			
								D_{16}	D_{20}	D_{24}			
4.	—2.000			.206	—.202	—.124		.757	—.066	.106	.197	.128	2 9
	(−8.746)			(2.663)**	(−2.576)*	(—1.797)†		(2.541)*	(—.954)	(.927)			

Values in brackets give '*t*' values
*Significant at 5 per cent level of significance
**Significant at 1 per cent level of significance
†Significant at 10 per cent level of significance

TABLE 5.6-C: **Multiple regression analysis: 1971-72**

Dependent Variable: Log $(L_{lj}/\sum_i L_{ij})$

(1) *Administrative, executive and managerial workers* (*No. of observations 81*)

	Log (K/X)	Log (L_l/X)	Log (K/L)	Log (E/I)	Log (X/F_n)	Intercept Dummy (δ)	Slope Dummies (γ)	R^2	$\bar{R}^2$	F
All industries										
1.	—1.079				—.207			.197	.186	19.3
	(—7.317)				(—4.396)**					
2.	—.777	—.573			—.451			.330	.313	19.2
	(—4.992)	(3.943)**			(—5.974)**					
3.	—1.200		.226	—.113	—.286			.339	.313	18.9
	(—6.351)		(2.888)**	(—1.564)	(—5.247)**					
Agriculture based industries										
							D_{21}			
4.	—.926				—.286		.067	.276	.257	14.9
	(—6.163)				(—5.402)**		(2.924)**			
Mining and metals based industries										
							D_{22}			
5.	—.898				—.277		.001	.291	.273	16.0
	(—5.985)				(—5.592)**		(3.225)**			

Chemicals based industries

					D_3			
6.	—.953			—.258	.219	.261	.242	13.8
	(—6.342)			(—5.214)**	(2.610)**			
					D_3			
7.	—1.120	.181	—.115	—.308	.174	.317	.281	8.8
	(—5.913)	(2.275)*	(—1.621)	(—5.648)**	(2.036)*			

Values in brackets give '*t*' values

*Significant at 5 per cent level of significance

**Significant at 1 per cent level of significance

turned out to be statistically significant.[13] This is also true for different groups of industries.

Some improvement is, however, seen when the results are obtained for 1966-67. Even these results do not suggest any meaningful relationship except in case of mining and metals based, and engineering industries, for which an inverse relationship between these skills and the degree of automation (E/I) is observed.

More interesting results are obtained for 1971-72 (Table 5.6-C). Unlike the previous two cross-sections, these results are encouraging. Specifically, the variable representing the scale of production (X/F_n) turns out to be an important determinant. Since the coefficient of X/F_n is statistically significant at the 1 per cent level with a minus sign, there is a possibility that an increase in the scale of production would tend to reduce the share of the skills included in this occupation division.

In addition to the scale of production, we observe from Table 5.6-C that the labour-output ratio (L/X) is also important in explaining the variation in the proportions of managerial workers. When both the variables (i.e., X/F_n and L/X) are used together, we find that the explanatory power of the equation in terms of the R^2 is improved considerably (e.g., from .197 in equation 1 to .330 in equation 2) (see Table 5.6-C). However, the coefficient of X/F_n is sensitive to the specification.

Our results for 1971-72 also suggest inter-group differences in the pattern of employment of these skills. It is, therefore, necessary to deal explicitly with the problem of heterogeneity in the sample of industries while forecasting demand for the managerial skills.

(Div. 2) **Clerical skills**

As compared to the managerial and executive workers, we find that the share of clerical workers in the total employment seems more strongly correlated with economic and technological variables used in this analysis (see Tables 5.7-A, B and C). At least, one variable, i.e. K/L, remains statistically significant for all the three cross-sections. Given its positive

TABLE 5.7-A: **Multiple regression analysis: 1963-64**

Dependent Variable: Log $(L_{ij}/\sum_i L_{ij})$

(2) *Clerical workers* (*No. of observatians 81*)

		Log (K/X)	Log (L/X)	Log (K/L)	Log (E/I)	Log (X/F_n)	Intercept Dummy (δ)	Slope Dummies (γ)			R^2	$\bar{R}^2$	F
All industries													
1.	—1.452	.135			—.020	.145					.133	.099	3.9
	(—7.348)	(1.391)			(—.274)	(2.908)**							
2.	—1.178		—.336								.138	.128	12.7
	(—19.464)		(—3.566)**										
3.	—1.331			.180	—.028	.065					.173	.141	5.4
	(—7.143)			(2.409)*	(—.648)	(1.090)							
Mining and metals based industries													
								D_{14}	D_{18}	D_{22}			
4.	—1.255			.202	—.034	.030		.001	—.167	—.193	.238	.176	3.8
	(−6.734)			(2.543)*	(−.518)	(.496)		(.026)	(−1.693)†	(−2.332)*			

Values in brackets give '*t*' values

*Significant at 5 per cent level of significance

**Significant at 1 per cent level of significance

†Significant at 10 per cent level of significance

TABLE 5.7-B: **Multiple regression analysis: 1966-67**

Dependent Variable: Log $(L_{ij}/\sum_i L_{ij})$

(2) Clerical workers *(No. of observations 77)*

	Log (K/X)	Log (L/X)	Log (K/L)	Log (E/I)	Log (X/F_n)	Intercept Dummy (δ)	Slope Dummies (γ)		R^2	$\bar{R}^2$	F
All industries											
1.	—1.490	.244		—.064	.116				.277	.247	9.3
	(—9.601)	(3.923)**		(—1.119)	(2.960)**						
2.	—1.176	—.231							.100	.087	8.2
	(—21.020)	(—2.869)*									
3.	—1.361		.195	—.037	.043				.272	.243	9.1
	(—8.894)		(3.852)**	(—.670)	(.954)						
4.	—1.432				.134				.122	.110	10.4
	(—11.272)				(3.222)**						
Agriculture based industries											
							D_9	D_{17}			
5.	—1.133	—.204		.006			—.021	.311	.184	.139	4.1
	(—11.271)	(—2.558)*		(.110)			(—1.293)	(2.109)*			

Chemicals based industries									
						D_{23}			
6. —1.443				.130		.274	173	.151	7.8
(—11.556)				(3.208)**		(2.155)*			
Engineering industries									
					D_4				
7. —1.198	—.220				.155		.189	.167	8.6
(—22.200)	(—2.855)**				(2.874)**				
					D_4				
8. —1.394				.114	.131		.184	.162	8.3
(—11.224)				(2.756)**	(2.374)*				
					D_4				
9. —1.311		.186	—.024	.028	.118		.322	.285	8.6
(—8.724)		(3.755)**	(—.455)	(.626)	(2.300)*				

Values in brackets give '*t*' values

*Significant at 5 per cent level of significance

**Significant at 1 per cent level of significance

TABLE 5.7-C: **Multiple regression analysis: 1971-72**

Dependent Variable: Log $(L_{ij}/\sum_i L_{ij})$

(2) *Clerical workers* (*No. of observations 81*)

	Log (K/X)	Log (L/X)	Log (K/L)	Log (E/I)	Log (X/F_n)	Intercept Dummy (δ)	Slope Dummies (γ)			R^2	$\bar{R}^2$	F
All industries												
1.	—1.152	.141		.044	.047					.118	.084	3.4
	(—7.691)	(2.519)*		(.820)	(1.341)							
2.	—1.064		.236	.016	—.057					.229	.200	7.6
	(—7.996)		(4.280)**	(.314)	(—1.480)							
Agriculture based industries												
						D_1	D_{13}	D_{17}	D_{21}			
3.	—.982		.313	.043	—.071	—.065	—.151	—.084	—.031	.306	.240	4.6
	(—7.078)		(4.667)**	(.792)	(—1.800)†	(—1.482)	(—2.667)**	(—.520)	(—1.629)			
Engineering industries												
						D_4						
4.	—1.017		.235	.023	—.076	.129				.300	.262	8.1
	(—7.889)		(4.449)**	(.487)	(—2.031)*	(2.753)**						

Values in brackets give '*t*' values

*Significant at 5 per cent level of significance

**Significant at 1 per cent level of significance

†Significant at 10 per cent level of significance

sign, it indicates that the demand for these workers will increase with an increase in the K/L. Also, the sign remains unchanged in different samples and formulations.

Surprisingly, we notice from Table 5.7-C that the coefficient of X/F_n yields a negative sign when used with K/L ratios. However, with the only exception of engineering industries, its coefficient is nowhere statistically different from zero. For the group of engineering industries when X/F_n is used with X/L and E/I, the coefficients of the two variables (i.e., X/F_n and K/L) turn out to be statistically significant at the 5 per cent and 1 per cent levels with a negative and positive sign, respectively (see Table 5.7-C, equation 4). It suggests that with an increase in scale of production, the proportion of clerical workers in the total employment would decline. However, with an increase in capital per unit of labour, the opposite may happen.

(Div. 3) **Sales workers**

The results in Tables 5.8-A, B and C are, by and large, not stable over different points of time. For example, while L/X is an important determinant of the share of this occupation in 1963-64, the scale of production (X/F_n) becomes important in 1966-67, and in the third cross-section, the coefficients of both L/X and X/F_n are statistically significant at the 1 per cent and 5 per cent levels, respectively. However, the sign of X/F_n changes in 1971-72. The implication is that while in the second cross-section (i.e. 1966-67), scale exerted a positive influence, the influence becomes negative in the third cross-section. An interesting point to note in the second cross-section is that there is an inverse relationship between the share of sales workers and the capital-labour (K/L) ratios. However, except for the engineering industries, the coefficient of this variable remains statistically not significant. In case of engineering industries, the coefficient is significant only at the 10 per cent level (see equation 6 in Table 5.8-B). Also this is not true for the first and the third cross-sections.

Compared to 1963-64, we observe from Tables 5.8-B and C that the coefficients of the dummy variables diminish over

TABLE 5.8-A: **Multiple regression analysis: 1963-64**

Dependent Variable: $\text{Log}\,(L_{ij}/\sum_i L_{ij})$

(3) *Sales workers* *(No. of observations 81)*

		Log (K/X)	Log (L/X)	Log (K/L)	Log (E/I)	Log (X/F_n)	Intercept Dummy (δ)	Slope Dummies (γ)			R^2	$\bar{R}^2$	F
	All industries												
1.	—3.219		—.851								.094	.082	8.2
	(—16.849)		(—2.863)**										
	Agriculture based industries												
							D_1						
2.	—3.542		—1.105				.407				.151	.129	6.9
	(—15.182)		(—3.365)**				(2.294)*						
							D_1	D_{13}	D_{17}	D_{21}			
3.	—2.911			.805	.114	—.137	.527	—.322	—2.332	.277	.314	.248	4.8
	(—5.161)			(2.992)**	(.557)	(—.762)	(2.855)**	(—1.210)	(—3.857)**	(3.289)**			
	Mining and metals based industries												
								D_6	D_{18}	D_{22}			
4.	—3.007	.336			.032			—1.035	—1.321	.729	.827	.229	4.9
	(—5.229)	(1.134)			(.148)			(—3.208)**	(—4.550)**	(2.888)**			

Chemicals based industries											
						D_7	D_{19}	D_{23}			
5.	—2.859	.601		.172	.035	.997	.678	.182	.207	.142	3.2
	(—4.696)	(1.778)†		(.752)	(.225)	(3.572)**	(2.945)**	(2.085)*			
Engineering industries											
						D_{12}	D_{20}				
6.	—3.119		—1.360	—.070		.778	.933		.220	.179	5.4
	(−6.500)		(—3.496)**	(—.349)		(2.261)*	(2.987)**				

Values in brackets give '*t*' values

*Significant at 5 per cent level of significance

**Significant at 1 per cent level of significance

†Significant at 10 per cent level of significance

TABLE 5.8-B: **Multiple regression analysis: 1966-67**

Dependent Variable: $\text{Log}\,(L_{ij}/\sum_i L_{ij})$

(3) *Sales workers* (*No. of observations 77*)

	Log (K/X)	Log (L/X)	Log (K/L)	Log (E/I)	Log (X/F_n)	Intercept Dummy (δ)	Slope Dummies (γ)			R^2	$\bar{R}^2$	F
All industries												
1.	—5.873	—.109		—.557	.794					.111	.074	3.0
	(—5.217)	(—.243)		(—1.395)	(2.797)**							
2.	—5.969		—.549	—.433	1.031					.138	.102	3.9
	(—5.476)		(—1.519)	(—1.112)	(3.210)**							
Agriculture based industries												
						D_1	D_{13}	D_{17}	D_{21}			
3.	—5.033		—.055	.085	.841	.401	—1.242	—1.107	.133	.294	.223	4.1
	(—4.706)		(—1.537)	(.216)	(2.744)**	(1.239)	(—2.980)**	(—1.030)	(.926)			
Mining and metals based industries												
						D_2						
4.	—4.678		—.481	.003	.872	—1.327				.264	.224	6.5
	(—4.341)		(—1.428)	(.009)	(2.884)**	(—3.525)**						

					D_{14}	D_{18}	D_{22}			
5.	−4.993	—.612	—.280	.840	.974	—.595	—.070	.291	.230	4.8
	(—4.772)	(—1.748)†	(—.768)	(2.770)**	(3.460)**	(—1.028)	(—1.257)			
Engineering industries										
					D_{16}	D_{20}	D_{24}			
6.	−5.093	—.353	—.615	.544	.688	—.601	—.182	.331	.274	5.8
	(—4.850)	(—.997)	(−1.704)†	(1.711)†	(4.157)**	(—1.879)†	(—.348)			

Values in brackets give '*t*' values

*Significant at 5 per cent level of significance

**Significant at 1 per cent level of significance

†Significant at 10 per cent level of significance

TABLE 5.8-C: **Multiple regression analysis: 1971-72**

Dependent Variable: Log $(L_{ij}/\sum_i L_{ij})$

(3) *Sales workers* (*No. of observations 81*)

	Log (K/X)	Log (L/X)	Log (K/L)	Log (E/I)	Log (X/F_n)	Intercept Dummy (δ)	Slope Dummies (γ)			R^2	$\bar{R}^2$	F
All industries												
1.	—1.924	.339			—1.089					.166	.145	5.8
	(—1.973)	(—3.725)**			(—2.304)*							
Agriculture based industries												
						D_1						
2.	—4.178	—2.078		.282		.782				.159	.126	4.9
	(—5.441)	(—3.700)**		(.634)		(2.802)**						
Mining and metals based industries												
							D_{14}	D_{18}	D_{22}			
3.	—5.190		.672	—1.193	—.077		3.411	—.619	—.001	.220	.146	2.9
	(—3.833)		(1.339)	(—2.124)*	(—.228)		(3.625)**	(—.536)	(—.317)			

Values in brackets give '*t*' values

*Significant at 5 per cent level of significance

**Significant at 1 per cent level of significance

time suggesting that inter-industry differences can be adequately represented in the form of technical and scale factors.

(Div. 4) **Farmers, fishermen, hunters, loggers, etc.**
This is a relatively unimportant occupational category for manufacturing industries. However, for the sake of completeness, the results are presented in Tables 5.9-A, B and C. These tables suggest that the estimated relationships are not stable over time. In 1963-64 and 1971-72, we observe a positive relationship between the share of the underlying skills and the *K/L* ratio. The coefficient is significant in most of the cases at the 1 per cent level for both the formulations, i.e., with and without the dummies. However, this relationship does not hold for 1966-67 as the *K/L* ceases to be statistically significant. Instead, *K/X* turns out to be significant at the 1 per cent level with a positive sign.

(Div. 5) **Mining, quarrymen and related workers**
Since the skills which constitute this occupation division include workers who are mainly involved in mining and quarrying operations, there is a possibility that the pattern of demand for workers with these skills would be different for the mining and quarry based industries from the rest. The results of the estimated relationships with intercept and slope dummies confirm this. We describe these results below.

Let us first present the results at the aggregate level. We notice from Tables 5.10-A, B and C that, compared to 1963-64, the estimates of the coefficients obtained for 1966-67 and 1971-72 reflect stronger technological relationship with the skills in question. While none of the explanatory variables except the dummies are significant for 1963-64, this is not true for the later cross-sections. For example, in 1966-67 the variable representing automation in production (*E/I*) becomes statistically significant at the 1 per cent level. This variable is significant at the 5 per cent level when used in conjunction with *K/L* and X/F_n (see equation 3, Table 5.10-B). In 1971-72, however, this variable is replaced by the *K/X* and *K/L*. The statistical significance of these variables at the 5 per cent level

TABLE 5.9-A: **Multiple regression analysis: 1963-64**

Dependent Variable: Log $(L_{ij}/\sum_i L_{ij})$

(4) *Farmers, fishermen, hunters, loggers, etc.* (*No. of observations 81*)

	Log (K/X)	Log (L/X)	Log (K/L)	Log (E/I)	Log (X/F_n)	Intercept Dummy (δ)	Slope Dummies (γ)				R^2	$\bar{R}^2$	F
	All industries												
1.	—2.587 (—4.398)		.553 (2.342)*	.037 (.176)	—.149 (—.791)						.089	.045	2.5
	Agriculture based industries												
2.	—2.834 (—4.815)		.649 (2.751)**	.148 (.683)	—.090 (—.480)	D_1 .393 (2.070)*					.138	.092	3.0
3.	—2.592 (—4.335)		.943 (3.305)**	.204 (.935)	—.187 (—.978)	D_1 .395 (2.021)*	D_{13} —.236 (—.838)	D_{17} —1.353 (—2.112)*	D_{21} .027 (.304)		.189	.111	2 4
	Chemicals based industries												
4.	—2.481 (—4.254)		.906 (3.382)**	.110 (.507)	—.178 (—.962)	D_3 1.022 (1.681)†	D_{15} —.146 (—1.784)†	D_{19} —1.253 (—2.339)*	D_{23} —.734 (—.901)		.180	.101	2.3
	Engineering industries												
5.	—2.634 (—4.149)	.628 (2.101)*		.363 (1.434)	.015 (.087)	D_4 —.735 (—1.448)	D_8 —.331 (—2.323)*	D_{20} —.236 (—1.091)	D_{24} —1.793 (—2.543)*		.180	.101	2.3

Values in brackets give '*t*' values

*Significant at 5 per cent level of significance

**Significant at 1 per cent level of significance

†Significant at 10 per cent level of significance

TABLE 5 9-B: **Multiple regression analysis: 1966-67**

Dependent Variable: Log $(L_{ij}/\sum_i L_{ij})$

(4) *Farmers, fishermen, hunters, loggers, etc.* (*No. of observations 77*)

		Log (K/X)	Log (L/X)	Log (K/L)	Log (E/I)	Log (X/F_n)	Intercept Dummy (δ)	Slope Dummies (γ)			R^2	$\bar{R}^2$	F
	All industries												
1.	—3.174	2.602			.018	.034					.275	.246	9.2
	(—2.296)	(4.691)**			(.037)	(.098)							
	Chemicals based industries												
							D_3	D_7	D_{19}	D_{23}			
2.	—4.144	3.693			−.626	.109	2.360	−.793	—1.765	—3.006	.358	.293	5.5
	(—2.924)	(5.458)**			(—1.157)	(.300)	(1.778)†	(−1.437)	(—1.759)†	(—2.302)*			

Values in brackets give '*t*' values

*Significant at 5 per cent level of significance

**Significant at 1 per cent level of significance

†Significant at 10 per cent level of significance

TABLE 5.9-C: **Multiple regression analysis: 1971-72**

Dependent Variable: Log $(L_{ij}/\sum_i L_{ij})$

(4) *Farmers, fishermen, hunters, loggers, etc.* (*No. of observations 81*)

	Log (K/X)	Log (L/X)	Log (K/L)	Log (E/I)	Log (X/F_n)	Intercept Dummy (δ)	Slope Dummies (γ)			R^2	$\bar{R}^2$	F
All industries												
1.	—2.054		1.342	.153	—.554					.104	.067	3.0
	(—1.735)		(2.738)**	(.338)	(—1.620)							
Mining and metals based industries												
						D_2	D_{14}	D_{18}	D_{22}			
2.	—3.091		1.313	—.527	—.510	2.813	2.775	—.502	—.002	.226	.152	3.0
	(—2.290)		(2.626)**	(—.941)	(—1.512)	(2.180)*	(2.960)**	(—.437)	(—.463)			

Values in brackets give 't' values

*Significant at 5 per cent level of significance

**Significant at 1 per cent level of significance

and that of E/I at the 10 per cent level in Table 5.10-C suggests that some of the explanatory power of E/I is taken away by them. Since the coefficients of these variables are positive, complementarity between the share of mining and quarrymen and these variables is implied.

Judging from the significance of intercept and slope dummies for all the three cross-sections, it might be inferred that the skills in question are industry specific. Thus, differences in their pattern of demand for different groups of industries ought not to be overlooked.

(Div. 6) **Workers in transport and communication occupations**

Since many of the skills aggregated here are crucial to the industrial sector, the poor results for 1971-72 are somewhat surprising (Table 5.11-C). This is, however, not the case with the earlier cross-sections. For instance, we observe from Table 5.11-A that in 1963-64 the share of employment in this occupation and the technical and scale factors, in particular, the K/X, E/I, K/L and X/F_n were positively related. Their coefficients were statistically significant at the 1 per cent level. The significance of L/X in 1963-64 at the 1 per cent level with a negative sign implies that industries with higher labour productivity tend to employ more of these skills.

The results are less encouraging when these relationships are estimated with the 1966-67 data. Table 5.11-B shows that only K/X and X/F_n turn out to be statistically significant at the 1 per cent and 5 per cent levels, respectively. Both the coefficients have a positive sign. The explanatory power of the equation, however, improves with the inclusion of dummy variables (see equations 2 and 3, Table 5.11-B). Note that unlike 1963-64, the slope dummies in 1966-67 perform better than those of the intercept dummies.

The results for the third cross-section (i.e., 1971-72) are pretty discouraging. None of the equations performed satisfactorily.

TABLE 5.10-A: **Multiple regression analysis: 1963-64**

Dependent Variable: Log $(L_{ij}/\sum_i L_{ij})$

(5) Mining and quarrymen (*No. of observations 81*)

	Log (K/X)	Log (L/X)	Log (K/L)	Log (E/I)	Log (X/F_n)	Intercept Dummy (δ)	Slope Dummies (γ)	R^2	$\bar{R}^2$	F
All industries										
1.	−3.966	.496			.119	.208		.085	.054	2.5
	(−6.285)	(1.592)			(.497)	(1.305)				
2.	−3.165		−.308		.346			.048	.024	2.0
	(−8.516)		(−.990)		(1.674)†					
3.	−3.614			.333	.200	.064		.081	.045	2.3
	(−5.891)			(1.351)	(.893)	(.341)				
Mining and metals based industries										
							D_2			
4.	−4.556	.483			−.146	.223	.985	.274	.236	7.2
	(−7.820)	(1.723)†			(−.655)	(1.554)	(4.403)**			
							D_2			
5.	−4.215			.309	−.062	.092	.981	.265	.226	6.8
	(−7.404)			(1.391)	(−.296)	(.522)	(4.357)**			

							D_{14}	D_{18}	D_{22}			
6.	–3.779		.281	.175	.068		.811	–.023	.061	.316	.260	5.7
	(–6.864)		(1.200)	(.891)	(.383)		(–4.979)**	(–.078)	(.248)			
Chemicals based industries												
						D_3	D_{15}	D_{19}	D_{23}			
7.	–4.021		.150	–.019	.071	–.264	.312	.352	1.145	.249	.177	3.5
	(–6.942)		(.564)	(–.089)	(.390)	(–.483)	(3.838)**	(.661)	(1.412)			
Engineering industries												
						D_4	D_8	D_{20}	D_{24}			
8.	–3.943	.430		–.198	.196	–.802	.407	.374	–.431	.188	.111	2.4
	(–6.013)	(1.393)		(–.758)	(1.110)	(–1.530	(2.768)**	(1.675)†	(–.529)			

Values in brackets give '*t*' values

*Significant at 5 per cent level of significance

**Significant at 1 per cent level of significance

†Significant at 10 per cent level of significance

TABLE 5.10-B: **Multiple regression analysis: 1966-67**

Dependent Variable: Log $(L_{ij}/\sum_{i} L_{ij})$

(5) *Mining and quarrymen* (*No. of observations 77*)

		Log (K/X)	Log (L/X)	Log (K/L)	Log (E/I)	Log (X/F_n)	Intercept Dummy (δ)	Slope Dummies (γ)	R^2	$\bar{R}^2$	F
	All industries										
1.	—3.529	1.392			2.376	—.085			.119	.083	3.3
	(—1.167)	(1.148)			(2.139)*	(—.111)					
2.	—3.675		—1.094		2.854				.111	.087	4.6
	(—2.035)		(—.767)		(2.877)**						
3.	—2.747			1.656	2.348	—.740			.138	.102	3.9
	(—.934)			(1.698)†	(2.232)*	(—.853)					
	Agriculture based industries										
							D_1				
4.	—2.247	.778			1.365	—.604	—2.761		.237	.194	5.6
	(—.785)	(.675)			(1.258)	(—.826)	(—3.328)**				
	Mining and metals based industries										
							D_2				
5.	—6.933			1.434	.931	—.223	4.300		.321	.283	8.5
	(—2.480)			(1.642)	(.937)	(—.284)	(4.405)**				

6.	−6.237 (—2.345)		2.046 (2.298)*	1.796 (1.938)†	—.053 (—.070)		D_{14} —3.035 (—4.241)**	D_{18} 3.171 (2.153)*	D_{22} 1.585 (1.109)	.371	.318	6.9
Chemicals based industries												
7.	—3.662 (—1.271)		2.311 (2.341)*	2.434 (2.382)*	—.429 (—.503)	D_3 —2.774 (—2.344)*				.200	.154	4.5
8.	−6.257 (−2.414)		.517 (.497)	1.330 (1.407)	—.134 (—.181)		D_{15} 1.568 (4.736)**	D_{19} —.123 (—.136)	D_{23} 6.748 (2.995)**	.415	.365	8.3
Engineering industries												
9.	—5.333 (—3.395)	—1.587 (—1.046)		1.471 (1.608)		D_4 3.120 (3.383)	D_{12} —6.375 (—4.563)**	D_{20} —.175 (—.204)				

Values in brackets give 't' values

*Significant at 5 per cent level of significance

**Significant at 1 per cent level of significance

†Significant at 10 per cent level of significance

TABLE 5.10-C: **Multiple regression analysis: 1971-72**

Dependent Variable: $\text{Log}\,(L_{ij}/\sum_{i} L_{ij})$

(5) *Mining and quarrymen* (*No. of observations 81*)

		Log (K/X)	Log (L/X)	Log (K/L)	Log (E/I)	Log (X/F_n)	Intercept Dummy (δ)	Slope Dummies (γ)			R^2	$\bar{R}^2$	F
All industries													
1.	—4.931	2.928			1.883	.446					.172	.140	5.3
	(—1.771)	(2.812)**			(1.875)†	(.683)							
2.	—2.785			2.483	1.968	—.804					.142	.108	4.2
	(—1.034)			(2.226)*	(1.908)†	(—1.034)							
Agriculture based industries													
							D_1						
3.	—3.378	2.892			.593	—.231	—3.091				.320	.284	8.9
	(—1.315)	(3.046)**			(.611)	(—.374)	(—4.073)**						
							D_1	D_5	D_{17}	D_{21}			
4.	—4.436	1.162			.594	.357	—3.770	2.230	4.377	—.870	.382	.322	6.4
	(—1.735)	(.649)			(.619)	(.540)	(—4.768)**	(1.037)	(1.448)	(—2.653)**			

Mining and metals based industries												
					D_2						
5.	—8.042	2.932	.733	.746	.324				.269	.230	7.0
	(—2.861)	(2.978)**	(.720)	(1.194)	(3.172)**						
					D_2	D_6	D_{18}	D_{22}			
6.	—9.077	2.869	.134	1.255	2.103	3.263	.788	—.003	.357	.295	5.8
	(—3.294)	(3.014)**	(.135)	(1.879)†	(2.000)*	(3.100)**	(.323)	(—.375)			
Engineering industries											
					D_4						
7.	—3.733	2.816	2.092	—.023	3.018				.275	.237	7.2
	(—1.410)	(2.870)**	(2.207)*	—.037	(3.296)**						
					D_4	D_8	D_{20}	D_{24}			
8.	—4.881	2.949	.080	.072	1.496	2.030	1.509	.704	.378	.318	6.3
	(—1.820)	(3.167)**	(.074)	(.106)	(.352)	(3.460)**	(1.640)	(.144)			

Values in brackets give 't' values

*Significant at 5 per cent level of significance

**Significant at 1 per cent level of significance

†Significant at 10 per cent level of significance

TABLE 5.11-A: **Multiple regression analysis: 1963-64**

Dependent Variable: $(L_{ij}/\sum_i L_{ij})$

(6) *Workers in transport and communication* (*No. of observations 81*)

		Log (K/X)	Log (L/X)	Log (K/L)	Log (E/I)	Log (X/F_n)	Intercept Dummy (δ)	Slope Dummies (γ)	R^2	$\bar{R}^2$	F
	All industries										
1.	—2.833 (—8.662)	.513 (3.177)**			.055 (.440)	.297 (3.588)**			.302	.275	11.1
2.	—1.851 (—9.020)		—.498 (—2.900)**		.301 (2.658)**				.172	.151	8.1
3.	−2.460 (−7.717)			.382 (2.982)**	.125 (1.083)	.134 (1.308)			.292	.264	10.6
	Engineering industries										
4.	−2.707 (—8.323)	.487 (3.073)**			.077 (.637)	.250 (2.987)**	D_4 .250 (2.125)*		.341	.306	9.8
5.			—.439 (—2.640)**		.306 (2.790)**		D_4 .332 (2.739)**		.246	.216	8.3
6.	—2.333 (−7.438)			.384 (3.094)**	.138 (1.229)	.079 (.778)	D_4 .282 (2.401)*		.342	.307	9.9

Values in brackets give 't' values

*Significant at 5 per cent level of significance

**Significant at 1 per cent level of significance

TABLE 5.11-B: **Multiple regression analysis: 1966-67**

Dependent Variable: Log $(L_{ij}/\sum_i L_{ij})$

(6) *Workers in transport and communication* (*No. of observations 77*)

	Log (K/X)	Log (L/X)	Log (K/L)	Log (E/I)	Log (X/F_n)	Intercept Dummy (δ)	Slope Dummies (γ)			R^2	$\bar{R}^2$	F
All industries												
1.	—3.490	1.416		—.087	.370					.320	.292	11.5
	(−4.734)	(4.790)**		(—.321)	(1.992)*							
Agriculture based industries							D_5	D_{17}	D_{21}			
2.	—3.860	.219		—.112	.526		2.496	—.130	.038	.509	.467	12.1
	(—5.886)	(.537)		(—.473)	(3.010)**		(4.695)**	(—.174)	(.472)			
Chemicals based industries							D_7	D_{19}	D_{23}			
3.	—3.988	1.974		—.390	.440		—.355	—.190	—1.919	.388	.336	7.4
	(—5.312)	(5.624)**		(—1.362)	(2.259)*		(—1.207)	(—.850)	(−2.764)**			

Values in brackets give 't' values

*Significant at 5 per cent level of significance

**Significant at 1 per cent level of significance

TABLE 5.11-C: **Multiple regression analysis: 1971-72**

Dependent Variable: Log $(L_{ij}/\sum_i L_{ij})$

(6) *Workers in transport and communication* (*No. of observations 81*)

		Log (K/X)	Log (L/X)	Log (K/L)	Log (E/I)	Log (X/F_n)	Intercept Dummy (δ)	Slope Dummies (γ)	R^2	$\bar{R}^2$	F
	All industries										
1.	−2.721	.558			.266	.305			.103	.068	2.9
	(—3.503)	(1.920)†			(.950)	(1.673)†					
2.	—1.878		—.556		.451				.069	.045	2.8
	(—3.768)		(—1.612)		(1.674)†						
3.	—2.341			.692	.221	—.016			.120	.085	3.1
	(—3.203)			(2.287)*	(.079)	(—.076)					

Values in brackets give '*t*' values

*Significant at 5 per cent level of significance

†Significant at 10 per cent level of significance

(Divs. 7 and 8) **Craftsmen and production process workers**

The results for these two occupational divisions are presented separately in Tables 5.12-A, B and C and 5.13-A, B and C. The two occupations are, however, combined in the interpretation of their results.

Since none of the equations of the first formulation, i.e., implying a common production function between all the industries under consideration, yields statistically significant relationships between the share of workers in these occupational divisions and the factors representing production technologies, we do not present their results. Instead, we have relied on the second formulation which explicitly considers technological differences (in terms of dummy variables) with the sample of industries. We observe from Tables 5.12 and 5.13 that the coefficients of intercept and slope dummies turn out to be statistically significant. This is true for both the occupational divisions and in each of the three cross-sections.

In case of the latter occupation (i.e., Div. 8) some of the variables, namely, E/I and X/F_n, turn out to be significant in the specification with the dummies. This is more clearly illustrated by the results for 1966-67 and 1971-72 (see Tables 5.13-B and C). Given the negative sign of the coefficient of XF_n, it may be inferred that an increase in the level of production tends to reduce the share of the workers in the total employment.

The significance of intercept and slope dummies indicates that the pattern of demand for skills comprising these occupations is different for different groups of industries.

(Div. 9) **Sports and recreation workers**

The results for this occupation are presented in Tables 5.14-A, B and C. We note that industries with the higher capital labour ratios have higher proportions of sports and recreation workers. This is confirmed by the results for all the three cross-sections. Considering that larger establishments, which are often capital intensive, have larger shares of these workers, we see no reason to question this result.

TABLE 5.12-A: **Multiple regression analysis: 1963-64**

Dependent Variable: Log $(L_{ij}/\sum_i L_{ij})$

(7) *Craftsmen and production process workers* (*No. of observations 81*)

	Log (K/X)	Log (L/X)	Log (K/L)	Log (E/I)	Log (F/X_n)	Intercept Dummy (δ)	Slope Dummies (γ)			R^2	$\bar{R}^2$	F
Mining and metals based industries												
						D_2	D_6	D_{18}	D_{22}			
1.	—.610	.101		.055	.089	—.431	—.574	..455	—.086			
	(—1.474)	(.484)		(.350)	(.836)	(—2.529)*	(—2.386)*	(2.154)*	(—.386)	.140	.058	1.7
Chemicals based industries												
							D_7	D_{19}	D_{20}			
2.	—.902	.316		—.053	.094		—.510	—.306	—.143	.118	.046	1.6
	(—2.214)	(1.400)		(—.345)	(.888)		(—2.730)**	(—1.983)*	(—.245)			
Engineering industries												
						D_4						
3.	—.566	.057		—.037	—.091	.395				.093	.046	1.9
	(—1.400)	(.291)		(.243)	(—.397)	(2.704)**						
						D_4						
4.	—.600	.102		.054		.393				.094	.058	2 6
	(—2.621)	(.530)		(.423)		(2.793)**						
						D_5						
5.	—.542		—.037	.071	—.024	.398				.093	.045	1.9
	(—1.389)		(—.237)	(.509)	(—.187)	(2.732)**						

Values in brackets give 't' values

*Significant at 5 per cent level of significance

**Significant at 1 per cent level of significance

TABLE 5.12-B: **Multiple regression analysis: 1966-67**

Dependent Variable: Log $(L_{ij}/\sum_i L_{ij})$

(7) *Craftsmen and production process workers* (*No. of observations 81*)

	Log (K/X)	Log (L/X)	Log (K/L)	Log (E/I)	Log (X/F_n)	Intercept Dummy (δ)	Slope Dummies (γ)			R^2	$\bar{R}^2$	F
Agriculture based industries												
							D_5	D_{17}	D_{21}			
1.	—.887	.680		.034	.084		—.806	—.362	—.109	.165	.094	2.3
	(—1.994)	(2.461)*		(.211)	(.707)		(—2.236)*	(—.715)	(—1.970)*			
Mining and metals based industries												
						D_2	D_6	D_{18}	D_{22}			
2.	—.700	.069		.107	.154	—.443	.522	.752	.251	.213	.134	2.7
	(—1.534)	(.383)		(.633)	(1.332)	(—2.637)**	(2.469)*	(3.095)**	(1.080)			
Engineering industries												
						D_4						
3.	—.530	.082		.091	—.033	.448				.131	.082	2.7
	(—1.191)	(.455)		(.557)	(—.295)	(2.930)**						
						D_4						
4.	—.425.		.234	.127		.466				.143	.107	4.1
	(—1.643)		(1.153)	(.896)		(3.272)**						

Values in brackets give 't' values

*Significant at 5 per cent level of significance

**Significant at 1 per cent level of significance

TABLE 5.12-C: **Multiple regression analysis: 1971-72**

Dependent Variable: Log $(L_{ij}/\sum_i L_{ij})$

(7) *Craftsmen and production process workers* (*No. of observations 81*)

	Log (K/X)	Log (L/X)	Log (K/L)	Log (E/I)	Log (X/F_n)	Intercept Dummy (δ)	Slope Dummies (γ)			R^2	$\bar{R}^2$	F
Mining and metals based industries												
						D_2	D_6	D_{18}	D_{22}			
1.	—.918	—.154		.058	.209	—.313	.544	.592	.001	.235	.162	3.2
	(—2.313)	(—1.124)		(.404)	(2.176)*	(—2.066)*	(3.589)**	(1.685)†	(.237)			
Chemicals based industries												
						D_3						
2.	—.824	—.140		.130	.501	—.377				.094	.055	2.0
	(—2.208)	(—1.964)		(.928)	(1.529)	(—2.308)*						
						D_3	D_7	D_{19}	D_{23}			
3.	—.802	—.161		.703	.132	—.692	—.336	.173	.697	.208	.132	2.7
	(—2.069)	(—.043)		(.503)	(1.364)	(—1.683)†	(—2.467)*	(.594)	(1.243)			
Engineering industries												
						D_3						
4.	—.506	—.181		.137	—.008	.465				.171	.128	3.9
	(—1.353)	(—1.309)		(1.029)	(—.095)	(3.600)**						
						D_4						
5.	—.535		.102	.098		.474				.157	.124	4.8
	(—2.273)		(.623)	(.772)		(3.720)**						

Values in brackets give 't' values

*Significant at 5 per cent level of significance

**Significant at 1 per cent level of significance

†Significant at 10 per cent level of significance

TABLE 5.13-A: **Multiple regression analysis: 1963-64**

Dependent Variable: Log $(L_{ij}/\sum_i L_{ij})$

(8) *Craftsmen and production process workers* (*No. of observations 81*)

	Log (K/X)	Log (L/X)	Log (K/L)	Log (E/l)	Log (X/F_n)	Intercept Dummy (δ)	Slope Dummies (γ)			R^2	$\bar{R}^2$	F
Engineering industries												
1.	—.344 (—1.683)	—.693 (—.696)		.125 (1.635)	.032 (.612)	D_4 —.284 (—3.833)**				.197	.155	4.6
2.	—.323 (—2.779)		—.640 (—.660)	.102 (1.582)		D_4 —.282 (—3.948)**				.192	.161	6.1
3.	—.320 (—1.449)	—.113 (—1.087)		.087 (.900)	.011 (.180)		D_8 —.043 (—.879)	D_{20} —.046 (—.616)	D_{24} .358 (2.788)**	.172	.105	2.6

Values in brackets give '*t*' values

**Significant at 1 per cent level of significance

TABLE 5.13-B: **Multiple regression analysis: 1966-67**

Dependent Variable: Log $(L_{ij}/\sum_i L_{ij})$

(8) *Craftsmen and production process workers* (*No. of observations* 77)

	Log (K/X)	Log (L/X)	Log (K/L)	Log (E/I)	Log (X/F_n)	Intercept Dummy (δ)	Slope Dummies (γ)			R^2	$\bar{R}^2$	F
All industries												
1.	−.006 (−2.476)	−.147 (−1.563)		.147 (1.688)†	−.066 (−1.112)					.063	.024	1.6
Mining and metals based industries												
2.	−.036 (−.161)	−.052 (−.580)		.109 (1.290)	−.135 (−2.344)*	D_2 .252 (2.994)**	D_6 −.369 (−3.483)**	D_{18} −.430 (−3.537)**	D_{22} −.078 (−.674)	.288	.215	4.0
3.	−.163 (−.706)	−.090 (−.956)		.186 (2.185)*	−.137 (−2.255)*		D_6 −.264 (−2.948)*	D_{18} −.341 (−2.740)**	D_{22} −.087 (−.713)	.195	.126	2.8
Chemicals based industries												
4.	−.064 (−.276)	−.150 (−1.617)		.125 (1.468)	−.100 (−1.787)†	D_3 .200 (2.215)*				,122	.074	2.5
5.	−.060 (−.251)	−.108 (−.971)		.129 (1.425)	−.114 (−1.848)†		D_7 .161 (1.729)†	D_{19} .143 (2.019)*	D_{23} −.256 (−1.164)	.181	.111	2.6

Engineering industries

						D_4			
6.	−.171	—.060		.091	−.024	—.289	.218	.175	5.1
	(—.769)	(−.658)		(1.115)	(—.423)	(—3.783)**			
						D_1			
7.	−.394		−.150	.053		—.315	.234	.203	7.4
	(—3.068)		(−1.481)	(.754)		(—4.442)**			

Values in brackets give '*t*' values
*Significant at 5 per cent level of significance
**Significant at 1 per cent level of significance
†Significant at 10 per cent level of significance

TABLE 5.13-C: **Multiple regression analysis: 1971-72**

Dependent Variable: Log $L_{ij}/\sum_{i} L_{ij}$)

(8) Craftsmen and production process workers *(No. of observations 81)*

	Log (K/X)	Log (L/X)	Log (K/L)	Log (E/l)	Log (X/F_n)	Intercept Dummy (δ)	Slope Dummies (γ)			R^2	$\bar{R}^2$	F
Agriculture based industries												
						D_1	D_5	D_{17}	D_{21}			
1.	—.051	—.079		.178	—.079	.148	.203	—.186	.076	.172	.093	2.2
	(—.211)	(—.465)		(1.962)*	(—1.265)	(1.983)*	(1.000)	(—.652)	(2.460)*			
						D_1	D_{17}	D_{17}	D_{21}			
2.	—.978		—.011	.128	—.102	.202	.145	—.228	.968	.185	.107	2.4
	(—.415)		(—.098)	(1.388)	(—1.524)	(2.709)**	(1.505)	(—.865)	(3.024)**			
Mining and metals based industries												
						D_2	D_6	D_{18}	D_{22}			
3.	—.017	.033		.124	—.162	.244	—.381	—.213	.001	.278	.209	4.0
	(—.072)	(.406)		(1.434)	(—2.796)**	(2.683)**	(—4.176)**	(—1.009)	(.523)			
Chemicals based industries												
						D_2	D_7	D_{19}	D_{23}			
4.	—.063	.057		.116	—.102	.416	.210	—.132	—.664	.238	.165	3.2
	(—.269)	(.614)		(1.369)	(—1.733)†	(1.669)†	(2.543)*	(—.745)	(—1.951)†			

Engineering industries

5.	—.241 (—1.109)	.053 (.668)		.072 (.934)	—.016 (—.303)	D_4 —.367 (—4.874)**	.268	.230	6.9
6.	—.315 (—2.318)		—.054 (—.577)	.078 (1.066)		D_4 —.377 (—5.132)**	.265	.237	9.3

Values in brackets give '*t*' values
*Significant at 5 per cent level of significance
**Significant at 1 per cent level of significance
†Significant at 10 per cent level of significance

TABLE 5.14-A: **Multiple regression analysis: 1963-64**

Dependent Variable: Log $(L_{ij}/\sum_{i} L_{ij})$

(9) *Sports and recreation workers* *(No. of observations 81)*

		Log (K/X)	Log (L/X)	Log(K/L)	Log (E/I)	Log (X/F_n)	Intercept Dummy (δ)	Slope Dummies (γ)	R^2	$\bar{R}^2$	F
All industries											
1.	—1.361	.247			.163	.039			.105	.070	3.0
	(—4.138)	(1.522)			(1.307)	(.474)					
2,	—1.288		—.337		.250				.126	.104	5.6
	(—6.878)		(—2.152)*		(2.457)*						
3.	—1.152			—.302	.157	—.094			.143	.109	4.3
	(—3.700)			(2.417)*	(1.387)	(—.942)					

Values in brackets give '*t*' values

*Significant at 5 per cent level of significance

TABLE 5.14-B: **Multiple regression analysis: 1966-67**

Dependent Variable: Log $(L_{ij}/\sum_i L_{ij})$

(9) *Sports and recreation workers* (*No. of observations* 77)

		Log (K/X)	Log (L/X)	Log (K/L)	Log (E/I)	Log (X/F_n)	Intercept Dummy(δ)	Slope Dummies (γ)	R^2	$\bar{R}^2$	F
	All Industries										
1.	—1. 443	.177			.045	.021			.123	.087	3.4
	(7.784)	(2.402)*			(.662)	(.455)					
2.	—1.319		—.090		.116				.061	.035	2.4
	(—11.664)		(—1.013)		(1.866)†						
3.	—1.345			.190	.048	—.053			.174	.140	5.1
	(—7.669)			(3.269)**	(.766)	(—1.028)					

Values in brackets give '*t*' values

*Significant at 5 per cent level of significance

**Significant at 1 per cent level of significance

†Significant at 10 per cent level of significance

TABLE 5.14-C: **Multiple regression analysis: 1971-72**

Dependent Variable: Log $(L_{ij}/\sum_i L_{ij})$

(9) *Sports and recreation workers* (*No. of observations 81*)

		Log (K/X)	Log (L/X)	Log (K/L)	Log (E/I)	Log (X/F_n)	Intercept Dummy (δ)	Slop Dummies (γ)			R^2	$\bar{R}^2$	F
All industries													
1.	—1.359	.213			.024	—.032					.107	.072	3.1
	(—6.379)	(2.674)**			(.318)	(—.641)							
2.	—1.232			.401	—.031	—.206					.290	.262	10.5
	(—6.827)			(5.369)**	(—.445)	(—3.954)**							
Agriculture based industries													
							D_1	D_9	D_{17}				
3.	—1.584		—.219		.087		.772	—.243	.261		.149	.092	2.6
	(—2.001)		(—1.814)†		(1.078)		(2.900)**	(—2.869)**	(1.268)				
Chemicals based industries													
								D_{15}	D_{19}	D_{22}			
4.	—1.229			.436	—.058	—.228		.006	.024	—.553	.331	.277	6.1
	(—6.427)			(4.770)**	(—.790)	(—4.285)**		(.219)	(.362)	(—1.871)†			

Values in brackets give '*t*' values

*Significant at 5 per cent level of significance

**Significant at 1 per cent level of significance

†Significant at 10 per cent level of significance

The scale variable (X/F_n) is, however, negatively related with these skills. But the coefficients of this variable remained statistically insignificant; the only exception being 1971-72.

With the only exceptions of the agriculture and the chemicals based industries in 1971-72, the coefficeints of intercept and slope dummies are nowhere statistically significant. This indicates that there is not much difference in the pattern of demand for these workers on account of inter-industry differences in their production technologies.

ASSESSMENT OF THE RESULTS

Some comments on the preceding analysis are given below.

1. Our experiments with the traditional method do not yield very satisfactory results. We note that the coefficients of certain variables change drastically in regressions for different years. Hence, from this analysis, it is difficult to determine which factors are empirically more relevant.
2. The share of non-production (or non-manual) workers seems to be more closely associated with the factors representing the production technology—the only exception being managerial workers. In addition to the technological factors, average output per unit of firm, used as a proxy for the scale of production, is an important determinant of the skills examined here, in general, and of non-production skills, in particular. Since in many cases, this variable is statistically different from unity, the assumption of constant returns to scale used in some earlier studies (e.g., Layard and Saigal, 1966) seems unwarranted.
3. The capital intensity variables and shares of serveral occupations are positively related.
4. The statistical significance of slope and intercept dummies confirms that there are important technological differences between industries in our sample. It, therefore, suggests that a straightforward application of the regression analysis treating each industry alike in terms

of the production function might be hazardous for occupational forecasting.

It might, therefore, be concluded that an application of the traditional method to cross-sectional data of the type used in this chapter is unlikely to yield predictive relationships on the basis of which projections of occupational structure could be attempted. Until more detailed time series data become available, it may be preferable to experiment with methods whose data requirements are relatively less.

REFERENCES

1. The overlap with section 1 of Chapter 3 is unavoidable as we will refer to the assumptions of this approach in our evaluation following the empirical results.
2. The specification here is similar to that adopted in the OECD (1970) study.
3. A list of industries for each sub-group is presented in Appendix 5.1 of this Chapter.
4. Following the general rule of exclusion, *m* categories can be distinguished by *m*—1 dummy variable. For a more detailed discussion, see Kmenta (1971).
5. Note that the number of observations in the second cross-section (i.e. 1966-67) is 77.
6. Since both the explained and explanatory variables in this exercise are in the form of ratios, the differences arising out of uneven coverage may not unduly bias the results.
7. It may be conjectured that these differences reflect no more than differences in the staffing patterns, or, alternatively, that these differences reflect differences in the underlying production functions. These issues unfortunately cannot be resolved with the data available to us at the time of this study. For some tentative results, see Gaiha (1974).
8. For these details, refer to Table 2.2.
9. The correspondence of the two classifications is shown in Appendix 5.1 of this Chapter.
10. To decide whether the coefficients are different from unity, the following null and alternative hypotheses (i.e H_N and H_A, respectively) are tested:

$$H_N : \beta = 1$$
$$H_A : \beta \neq 1$$

The test statistic is

$$\frac{|\hat{\beta}|-1}{6(\hat{\beta})}$$

11. The diversity of skills possessed by professional workers can be judged by the very fact that this occupation division lumps together development scientists, engineers, economists, doctors, jurists, creative artists, writers, etc. Many of these skills differ in terms of their educational requirements. It is, therefore, important from a policy view-point to analyse some of the more important skills separately.
12. Layard and Saigal (1966) have, for example, assumed constant returns to scale.
13. These results are not presented here.

APPENDIX 5.1

GROUP-WISE LIST OF INDUSTRIES AND CORRESPONDENCE OF SIC AND CSO INDUSTRIAL CLASSIFICATION

Sub-group 1: Agriculture based industries

Sl. No.	SIC Codes	CSO Codes	
1	200	205-1, 2	Production of rice, atta, flour. etc., by milling, dehusking of crops and foodgrains
2	201	207-1	Production of sugar and syrup in mills
3	202	207-2	Production of indigenous sugar and gur etc.
4	203	203	Production of fruit products, e.g., jam, jelly and sauce, etc.
5	205	206	Production of bread, biscuit and cake etc.
6	206	202-1, 2; 209-10	Production of butter, ghee, cheese and other dairy products
7	207	209-2	Production of edible fats and oils (o.t. vanaspati)
8	208	209-3	Production of hydrogenated oil (vanaspati)
9	209	208	Production of other food products, e.g., sweetmeat and condiments, chira, chocolate, etc.
10	217	209-4	Processing of tea in factories
11	220-26	220-1 to 220-6	Manufacture of tobacco products
12	230	239-1	Cotton ginning, cleaning, pressing and baling
13	231-36 (-33)	231-1	Cotton spinning in mills, powerlooms and handlooms, and manufacture of khadi textile in handlooms
14	239	233	Manufacture of cotton, cordage, rope and twine

15	240	239-2	Jute pressing and baling
16	241	231-2	Jute spinning and weaving
17	252-55	231-3	Wool spinning and weaving in mills, powerlooms and handlooms, etc.
18	260-64 (-61)	231-4	Spinning and weaving of silk textiles in mills, powerlooms and handlooms
19	270	231-9	Manufacture of carpet and other similar textile products
20	271	232	Manufacture of hosiery and other knitted fabrics and garments
21	273	243-1	Making of textile garments including raincoats and head gears
22	275	239-5, 6 and 8	Manufacture of water-proof textile products, such as oil cloth, tarpulin, etc.
23	277	239-4	Manufacture of coir and coir products
24	278	243-2	Manufacture of umbrella
25	279	239-7 and 9	Processing and manufacture of textile products (n.e.c.)
26	280	251-1	Sawing and planing of wood
27	281	260-1	Manufacture of wooden furniture and fixtures
28	290-91	271-1 to 4	Manufacture of pulp and paper in mills and handmade
29	292	271-5	Manufacture of paper products, such as paper bags, boxes, moulded pulp goods, etc.
30	310	291	Currying, tanning and finishing of hides and skins and preparation of finished leather
31	311	241	Manufacture of shoes and other leather footwear
32	313	293	Manufacture of leather products (excluding shoes and wearing apparel)
33	321	300-3	Manufacture of rubber footwear
34	322-323	300-2 and 4	Manufacture of rubber goods for industrial purposes and other rubber products from synthetic or natural rubber

Sub-group 2: Mining and metals based industries

Sl. No.	SIC Codes	CSO Codes	
1	325-26	329	Production of coal and its products
2	340	331-1 to 4	Manufacture of structural clay products
3	341	334 and 339-2	Manufacture of cement and cement products
4	343	339-5	Manufacture of structural stone goods
5	347	339-1	Manufacture of asbestos products
6	348	339-7	Manufacture of mica products
7	351	333-1	Manufacture of chinaware and crockery
8	359	339-8	Manufacture of other non-metallic mineral products
9	360	341-1	Manufacture of iron and steel
10	361	342	Manufacture including smelting, refining of non-ferrous metals and alloys
11	363	341-4	Manufacture of structural steel products
12	368	350-4 and 6	Enamelling, galvanising, plating and polishing of metal products
13	369	350-2, 3	Manufacture of sundry hardwares and sundry ferrous engineering products

Sub-group 3: Chemicals based industries

Sl. No.	SIC Codes	CSO Codes	
1	210-13	211, 12 and 13	Production of distilled spirits, wines, country liquor and indigenous liquor, etc.
2	320	300-1	Manufacture of tyres and tubes
3	324	321	Production of petroleum and its products in refineries
4	330	311-2.1, 2.2 and 311-10	Manufacture of basic industrial chemicals, such as acid, alkalis, etc.
5	331	311-7 and 313	Manufacture of dyes, paints and colour, etc.
6	332	311-1.1, 1.3	Manufacture of fertilizers
7	333	311-6	Manufacture of ammunition and explosives
8	334	319-8	Manufacture of matches
9	335	319-5 and 7	Manufacture of medicines and pharmaceutical preparations and cosmetics
10	346	319-6	Manufacture of soap and other washing compounds
11	337+39	311-3, 4, 8, 9, 12	Manufacture of turpentine, synthetic, and plastic products and other chemicals or their products (n.e.c.)
12	377	370-1.10	Manufacture of all kind of batteries

Sub-group 4: Engineering industries

Sl. No.	SIC Codes	CSO Codes	
1	370	360-4.2, 4.4 to 360-4.14 and 360-13	Manufacture and assembling of machinery (o.t. electrical) except textile machinery
2	371	360-1 and 360-9	Manufacture and assembling of prime movers and boilers (o.t. diesel engines, tractors, road rollers).
3	372	360-7	Manufacture of machine tools
4	373	360-4.1	Manufacture of textile machinery and accessories
5	374	370-1.1, 1.2	Manufacture of heavy electric machinery
6	375	370-1.3, 104	Manufacture of electric lamps and fans
7	376	370-1.6	Manufacture of insulated wires and cables
8	380	382-1	Manufacture, assembly and repairing of locomotives
9	381	382-2, 3	Manufacture of wagon, coaches and tramways, etc.
10	382	383	Manufacture and assembling of motor vehicles (except engines)
11	384	384	Repairing and servicing of motor vehicles
12	385+89	385 and 389	Manufacture of bicycles and tricycles and accessories and other transport equipment
13	386	381-1	Building and repairing of water transport equipment
14	387	386	Manufacture and repair of air transport equipment including planes and engines
15	391	391-1, 3	Manufacture of scientific, medical and surgical instruments

Sub-group 5: Miscellaneous industries

Sl. No.	SIC Codes	CSO Codes	
1	272	231-6	Embroidery and making of crepe lace and fringes
2	302-03	280-1, 2	All types of printings and bindings
3	354	332-5	Manufacture of glass apparatus
4	357	332-1, 2, 3 and 6	Manufacture of glass and glass products (excluding glass apparatus and optical and photographic lenses, etc.)
5	392	393	Assembling and repairing of watches and clocks
6	395	399-3, 4	Manufacture of stationery articles such as pencils, fountain pen, etc.
7	396	399-11	Manufacture of sports goods

6

AN ECONOMY-WIDE APPLICATION OF STRUCTURAL METHOD

First-order Markov Probability Model

AN ALTERNATIVE approach to the traditional method of manpower forecasting is the Markov probability formulation. The data requirements of this approach are modest. Given that there are very few developing countries for which detailed time series occupational data exist, this approach is sometimes recommended for forecasting the occupational structure in developing countries [see, for example, Sabolo (1971)]. In what follows, we present the results of several experimental formulations of the Markov probability approach with Indian data.

This chapter is organised as follows. First, the assumptions are described. Then the basic model is specified. And, finally, the results are discussed.

THE ASSUMPTIONS

This approach is distinguishable from the traditional method in two respects:

(*i*) the focus of the Markov probability approach is on inter-occupational movements as a determinant of temporal changes in the occupational structure of employment, and

(*ii*) the Markov probability approach explicitly takes into account the inter-dependence between the occupational categories.

From an estimation point of view, it is important to note that while in the traditional approach a direct relationship is premised between, say, technology and the occupational structure, in the Markov probability formulation, it would be mediated by changes in inter-occupational movements.[1]

THE MODEL

We postulate that the pattern of occupational mobility is generated by a system of simultaneous and stochastic relationship among the different occupational groups. Assuming also that these relationships are conditional upon a chain of lagged effects which influence the mobility of workers from one occupational group to another, a finite Markov probabilistic model is suggested in the literature.[2] Some of the basic features of this model are briefly described below.

A finite stochastic process of the Markov type is determined from two necessary conditions, namely, (*i*) that there are a set of finite number of states or outcomes (in our case, occupations) which a discrete random variable can take, and (*ii*) the outcome of a given trial is probabilistically conditional upon the immediately preceding trial. These conditions yield a first-order Markov chain system. If we further assume that the first-order condition (set out at the initial stage) holds at all the successive stages too, we obtain a stationary Markov process.[3] This is expressed as follows:

$$L_t . P = L_{t+1} \qquad \text{...(6.1)}$$

where L_t represents the row vector of employment by occupations (the number of occupations being n) of the order $(l \times n)$ at time (t), P is a transition matrix of the order $(n \times n)$, and each element of this matrix, P_{ij}, remains constant over time. The P_{ij}s in this case represent the probability of an individual shifting from occupation i at time (t) to occupation j at time $(t+1)$ such that,[4]

$$0 \leqslant P_{ij} \leqslant 1 \qquad \text{...(6.2)}$$

$$\sum_{j=1}^{n} P_{ij} = 1 \qquad \text{...(6.3)}$$

for $i = 1, 2, ..., n$

Since L_t in equation (6.1) is known *a priori*, we are required to estimate only the transition probabilities (hereafter referred to as *TP*s) to get the employment profile at $(t+1)$. It, however, raises some difficult estimation problem. An important point to note here is that there is very little information on inter-occupational movements. The time-series of occupational proportions are, therefore, used to estimate the *TP*s.

Given the assumption of a finite Markov-process and macro-level data, the *TP*s can either be estimated by using the Ordinary Least Square (OLS) method to a sequence of observations or with the help of quadratic or linear programming techniques (see, Lee, *et al*, 1965). Note that the OLS fails to ensure the two basic conditions of the formulation, namely, the non-negativity of the P_{ij}s and the requirement that row sum equals one. Alternatively, a method based on restricted least squares is suggested. It consists of replacing implausible values of TP matrix by extreme plausible values (i.e., 0 and 1) and then re-estimating the linear relations in which they appear. After all the 0 and 1 alternatives are exhausted, the specification, that minimises the residual sum of squares, is chosen.[5] However, when the number of implausible values in *TP* matrix is large, the adjustment procedure becomes complicated and the computational requirements exorbitant. We have chosen the linear programming formulation primarily because of its computational convenience.

Following Lee, *et al* (1965), the estimation of *TP*s is derived by minimising the sum of absolute deviation (U) subject to the constraints given in equations (6.2) and (6.3). The model is then written as,

Definition equation: $L_{t+1} = L_t \, . \, P + U_{t+1}$

Objective function: $\sum_{t=1}^{T-1} (U'_{t+1} + U''_{t+1}) \, . \, \text{I} \ldots\ldots \text{Min.}$

Constraints : $\sum_{j=1}^{n} P_{ij} = 1 \quad \forall_i$

$P_{ij} \geqslant 0 \quad \forall_i, \forall_j$

$\left.\begin{matrix} U'_{t+1} \geqslant 0 \\ U''_{t+1} \geqslant 0 \end{matrix}\right\} \quad \forall_t$

where

L_t =a vector of employment by occupation $(l \times n)$ expressed as a proportion of total employment in year t;

L_{t+1} =a vector of employment by occupation $(l \times n)$ expressed as a proportion of total employment in year $t+1$;

P=a matrix of transition probabilities with $P=(P_{ij})$ of the order $(n \times n)$;

U_{t+1}=a row vector of residuals between the observed L_{t+1} and $L_t \cdot P$. For computational purposes, U_{t+1} is expressed as the difference between U'_{t+1} and U''_{t+1};[6] and

I=represents an identity vector.

For projection purposes, given an initial occupational vector, the transition matrix (*TP*) is first raised to an appropriate power, and then post-multiplying the occupational vector by the transition matrix, the occupational projections are obtained. To illustrate, for example, if we want to project the employment profile for, say, 1985-86 from a given skill-mix vector of the year 1970-71, all that we have to do is to obtain $L_{70-71} \cdot P^{15}$.

It is suggested that a mobility index (M) can also be obtained from the *TP*. This index is defined as:

$$M=\frac{n}{t_r}-1 \qquad \ldots(6.4)$$

where n is the sum of probabilities off the diagonal and t_r stands for trace (i.e., sum of elements along the principal diagonal). The higher the value of M the greater is the degree of occupational mobility.

THE DATA

The time series of employment profile, used to estimate the model, is obtained from the published reports of the Directorate General of Employment and Training (D.G.E. & T.). Considering that the transition probabilities denote inter-occupational mobility of workers at the aggregate level—and not broken down by inter-sectoral movements—the occupational proportions at the aggregate level are obtained. We have combined the corresponding skills of the public and private sectors for the time-series of occupational proportions.[7] The time-series over the period 1960 to 1973 yields 7 observations. As the number of observations is small, occupational proportions at the disaggregated levels are not used. The following broad occupational divisions are considered:

1. Professional, technical and related workers (Div. 0)
2. Administrative, executive and managerial workers (Div. 1)
3. Clerical and sales workers (Div. 2+3)
4. Production process workers (excluding unskilled office and other workers) (Div. 4-9)
5. Unskilled workers (M. Groups 290, 414-15, 890, 899, 903, 931)

Note that the observed occupational classification differs slightly from that of the National Classification of Occupation (NCO, 1958). The pattern of classification followed by the NCO, 1958 does not include unskilled workers as a separate category at the one digit level. However, it needs to be emphasised that a distinction between skilled and unskilled workers is crucial for projection purposes. Hence, we have treated the unskilled workers as a separate category in the underlying analysis.

THE RESULTS

Three alternative specifications of the programming formulation are used. One specification is without any bounds and the remaining two are with bounds on P_{ij}s. Briefly, the bounds are designed to ensure that some of the P_{ij}s do not turn out to be implausibly, high or low. Since, as we noted earlier, very little is known about inter-occupational movements, the bounds are no more than guesses. The results of these models are presented in Tables 6.1, 6.2 and 6.3.

We note from the results in Tables 6.1, 6.2 and 6.3 that the value of the objective function is the lowest for the first specification, i.e., without any bounds. However, some of the P_{ij}s do not seem to be plausible. For instance, it is highly implausible that the clerical and sales workers would become unskilled workers in a year's time. It also seems somewhat unlikely that 14 per cent of the unskilled workers become clerical and sales workers and 55 per cent of them become production process workers over a period of one year (see Table 6.1).

To rule out such values, bounds are applied in the subsequent specifications. We note from Table 6.2 that as a result of the bounds some other P_{ij}s (to which the bounds do not apply) turn out to be implausible (e.g., P_{23}=.610). Hence, another specification with a different set of bounds is considered. The results of this specification given in Table 6.3 show that with a few exceptions the values of P_{ij}s are generally plausible. One of the exceptions is P_{13}=.122. It does not seem likely that over 12 per cent of the professional workers move into the category of clerical and sales workers during a year. It is interesting to note the positive relationship between the value of the objective function and the number of bounds. For instance, with an additional bound (P_{45}=0) the value of the objective function increases from .132 in Table 6.2 to .207 in Table 6.3. While it is necessary to use the bounds, it is worth emphasising that with an increase in their number, there is a loss of predictive power.

CONCLUSIONS

1. As far as the predictive power of the Markov probability approach is concerned, the models considered in this chapter performed well. The value of the objective function in each case is relatively low suggesting the close approximation of the projected values to the observed values.

2. However, a serious weakness of the model is that some elements of the transition matrix turn out to be implausible.

3. While the number of implausible values may be reduced through an increase in the number of prior bounds, this would reduce the predictive power of the model.

TABLE 6.1: **Transition probability matrix (P)**

(Without bounds)

Sl. No.	Rows	Columns: Profes-sional	Mana-gerial	Clerical & Sales	Prod. Process	Un-skilled
1.	Professional workers	0.800	0.025	0.175	0.0	0.0
2.	Managerial and executive workers	0.0	0.902	0.098	0.0	0.0
3.	Clerical and sales workers	0.0	0.0	0.050	0.0	0.950
4.	Production process workers	0.141	0.0	0.105	0.470	0.284
5.	Unskilled workers	0.0	0.0	0.144	0.546	0.310

Value of the objective function=0.0875

TABLE 6.2: **Transition probability matrix (P)**

(With bounds)

Sl. No.	Rows	Columns: Profes-sional	Mana-gerial	Clerical & Sales	Prod. Process	Un-skilled
1.	Professional workers	0.834	0.140	0.026	0.0	0.0
2.	Managerial and executive workers	0.0	0.390	0.610	0.0	0.0
3.	Clerical and sales workers	0.317	0.0	0.683	0.0	0.0
4.	Production process workers	0.0	0.0	0.035	0.441	0.524
5.	Unskilled workers	0.0	0.0	0.0	0.577	0.423

Value of the objective function=0.1317

Bounds

$P_{14}=0$ $P_{41}=0$
$P_{15}=0$ $P_{42}=0$
$P_{24}=0$ $P_{51}=0$
$P_{25}=0$ $P_{52}=0$
$P_{35}=0$ $P_{53}=0$

TABLE 6.3: **Transition probability matrix (P)**

(With bounds)

Sl. No.	Rows	Profes-sional	Mana-gerial	Clerical & Sales	Prod. Process	Un-skilled
1.	Professional workers	0.809	0.069	.122	0.0	0.0
2.	Managerial and executive workers	0.605	0.395	0.0	0.0	0.0
3.	Clerical and sales workers	0.173	0.093	0.692	0.042	0.0
4.	Production process workers	0.0	0.0	0.057	0.943	0.0
5.	Unskilled workers	0.0	0.0	0.0	0.025	0.975

Value of the objective function=0.2073

Bounds

$P_{14}=0$ $P_{41}=0$ $P_{53}=0$

$P_{15}=0$ $P_{42}=0$

$P_{24}=0$ $P_{45}=0$

$P_{25}=0$ $P_{51}=0$

$P_{35}=0$ $P_{52}=0$

REFERENCES

1. For an illustration, see Sabolo (1971), ILO (1971), etc.
2. Some important recent studies are ILO (1971), Sabolo (1971), Krishna (1974), Kadekodi and Gaiha (1976), Gaiha (1977), etc.
3. For a detailed discussion and derivation of the finite stationary Markov process, see Lee, Judge and Zellner (1970).
4. Since the elements of P_{ij} are non-negative and sum up to unity, the resulting $(n \times n)$ matrix.with an initial starting time (t), completely defines a Markov-chain process.
5. For a more detailed discussion and application of this method, see Telser (1963).
6. For more detailed exposition, see Lee *et al* (1965), p. 751.
7. Since the quality of data between public and private sectors vary sharply because of differences in their coverage and non-response rates, a prorata correction is made to the data on the lines suggested in section 2 of Chapter 4.

7

THE RAS ADJUSTMENT: MANUFACTURING SECTOR

WE HAVE seen in the previous chapters that neither the traditional nor the Markov probability formulation yielded very satisfactory results. Both of them are fraught with serious estimation problems which, given the scantiness of the data, cannot be easily overcome. We shall now present the results using the RAS adjustment method which requires minimal data.

This method of adjusting a matrix from given row and column totals was developed in the early forties. This was extensively used and refined in the Cambridge Growth Project (1963). Since then the RAS method has been widely used for a variety of matrix updating exercises, notably by Johansen (1968), Lecomber (1969), Parikh (1979), Dalvi (1981), etc.[1]

In the present analysis this method is used for determining changes in the structure of employment cross-classified by occupation and industry for different points of time. Its application to occupation-industry matrices for different points of time may help us in evaluating its potential usefulness for short and medium term forecasting. The scheme of our analysis is as follows. First, we will describe some of the properties of the RAS formulation. The data sources used to construct sector-wise occupation-industry matrices are presented next. This is followed by a discussion on our results which were worked out separately for the public and private sectors. In the final section, an assessment of the model for forecasting occupation-wise structure of employment is presented.

PROPERTIES OF THE RAS FORMULATION

Some of the properties of the RAS method are briefly described here.

Suppose that the inter-temporal variations in an occupation-industry flow matrix, A_{ij}, is governed through row (i.e., occupation) and column (i.e., industry-wise employment) effects interacting multiplicatively. Two matrices in the series are then related by

$$\hat{A}_{ij}^{t+k} = \hat{r}_i \, A_{ij}^{t} \, \hat{s}_j \qquad \text{...(7.1)}$$

where A_{ij} and $\hat{A}_{ij}$ are the base and the adjusted occupation-industry matrices $(m \times n)$ for years t and $t+k$, and $\hat{r}_j$ $(m \times m)$ and $\hat{s}_j$ $(n \times n)$ are the diagonal matrices of row and column multipliers.

Now suppose A_{ij}^{t} is known, and also the row and column totals for the terminal year $(t+k)$. Bacharach (1970) has shown that the adjusted matrix $\hat{A}_{ij}^{t+k}$ can then be easily derived by an iterative solution of the two equation systems given as:

$$\hat{r}_i \, A_{ij}^{t} \, s_j = \sum_j U_{ij}^{t+k} \qquad \text{...(7.2)}$$

$$r'_i \, A_{ij}^{t} \, \hat{s}_i = \sum_i V_{ij}^{t+k} \qquad \text{...(7.3)}$$

where U and V are the row and column totals of occupation-industry matrix for the year $(t+k)$ and known *a priori*, s is the column vector of the diagonal elements of $\hat{s}$, and r' is the column vector of the diagonal elements of $\hat{r}$. The subscripts i and j refer to the occupation and industry, respectively. The method involves a successive biproportional adjustment of the rows and columns of the base year's matrix (A_{ij}^{t}) until the constraints in equations (7.2) and (7.3) are simultaneously satisfied.[2]

So far the adjustment procedure was described in relation to a flow matrix. If, instead the adjustment it needed to a coefficient matrix, subject to row and column sum constraints, the method in question does not present any difficulty as a biproportional relationship between the flow matrices implies a bioproportional relationship between the coefficient matrices. Algebraically,

$$\hat{L}_{ij}^{t+k} = \hat{r}_i \, L_{ij}^{t} \, \hat{s}_j^{*} \qquad \ldots(7.4)$$

where L_{ji}^{t} and $\hat{L}_{ij}^{t+k}$ are the matrices of industry-wise occupational coefficients of the order $(m \times n)$, and $\hat{r}$ $(m \times m)$ and $\hat{s}^*$ $(n \times n)$ are the diagonal matrices of row and column multipliers, respectively. Note that the column multipliers, $\hat{s}^*$, are different from the multipliers for the flow matrices, $\hat{s}$. There is, however, a correspondence between the two sets of multipliers.[3] Since we are interested in adjusting coefficient matrices, it is the $\hat{s}^*$ which is relevant here.

Some features of the RAS are noted below:

(*i*) Zero elements in the base year matrix remain zero elements in the adjusted matrix.[4]

(*ii*) If the base year matrix is non-negative, the adjusted matrix is also non-negative.

(*iii*) It has been found that the method soon converges on the solution and, thus, not too demanding on computing time. Moreover, its data requirements are modest.

An important limitation of the RAS adjustment arises out of the 'even' spreading of changes along the rows and the columns. Let us illustrate this with an example. The elements of an occupation-industry matrix are subject to the column and row effects which would take the form of changes in industry and occupation-wise employment levels. Now, suppose that employment in an industry increases by 10 per cent. The column multiplier would then raise the elements in that column by 10 per cent. (The row constraint is being ignored to simplify the argument.) Since the skills of engineers or accountants are more expensive as compared to those of, say, clerical workers, a uniform increase in all occupations is highly unlikely. Similarly, on account of variation between industries in the capacity to employ highly skilled manpower a uniform increase in the elements of a row representing highly skilled professionals, associated with an increase in the row total in question, might also not come about easily.

However, our own results with Indian data suggest that the resulting discrepancies are not very serious.

ACCURACY OF THE RAS ADJUSTMENT

Let us now consider the accuracy of this method. While there is sufficient evidence which confirms the applicability of the RAS adjustment method, especially in the field of input-output analysis and international trade, it is not so far established that the method in question performs equally well in the areas like manpower demand projections. Bosworth *et al* (1974) and Gaiha (1977) have demonstrated its usefulness in manpower forecasting, but the evidence is somewhat limited to permit generalizations. We present here the results of much more detailed exercises.

Two competing hypotheses are tested here, namely (*i*) the 'same as before hypothesis' (hereafter referred to as the SAB hypothesis), and (*ii*) the RAS hypothesis. The SAB hypothesis premises that the occupational coefficients remain constant over time. Symbolically,

$$\frac{L_{ij}^{t+k}}{L_j^{t+k}} = \frac{L_{ij}^{t}}{L_j^{t}} \quad \forall_{i,j} \qquad ...(7.5)$$

or

$$\frac{L_{ij}^{t+k}}{L_j^{t+k}} - \frac{L_{ij}^{t}}{L_j^{t}} = 0 \quad \forall_{ij} \qquad ...(7.6)$$

where L_{ij} refers to the proportionate share of employees with occupation i in industry j. The superscripts t and $t+k$

are the time intervals with a time lag k. The RAS hypothesis, on the other hand, is that inter-temporal variations in industry-wise occupational coefficients are biproportional.

The test-statistics used to test for these hypotheses are presented in Table 7.1.[5]

TABLE 7.1: **Test-statistics for the SAB and the RAS hypotheses**

Test-Statistics	SAB Hypothesis	RAS Hypothesis
1. *ESS*	$\sum_i\sum_j (L_{ij}^{t+k} - L_{ij}^{t})^2$	$\sum_i\sum_j (L_{ij}^{t+k} - \hat{L}_{ij}^{t+k})^2$
2. *WESS*	$\sum_i\sum_j W_{ij} (L_{ij}^{t+k} - L_{ij}^{t})^2$	$\sum_i\sum_j W_{ij} (L_{ij}^{t+k} - \hat{L}_{ij}^{t+k})^2$
3. *WMESS*	$\sum_i\sum_j W_{ij} (L_{ij}^{t+k} - L_{ij}^{t})^2 / m\times n$	$\sum_i\sum_j W_{ij} (L_{ij}^{t+k} - \hat{L}_{ij}^{t+k})^2 / m\times n$
4. *WRMESS*	$\sqrt{\sum_i\sum_j W_{ij} (L_{ij}^{t+k} - L_{ij}^{t})^2 / m\times n}$	$\sqrt{\sum_i\sum_j W_{ij} (L_{ij}^{t+k} - \hat{L}_{ij}^{t+k})^2 / m\times n}$
5. Aggregate[6] chi-square (χ^2)	$\sum_i\sum_j A_{ij}^{t} \left(\frac{A_{ij}^{t+k}}{A_{ij}^{t}} - 1 \right)^2$	$\sum_i\sum_j A_{ij}^{t+k} \left(\frac{\hat{A}_{ij}^{t+k}}{A_{ij}^{t+k}} - 1 \right)^2$

Notations

L^t=actual occupation-industry coefficient matrix for year t

L^{t+k}=actual occupation-industry coefficient matrix for year $t+k$

$\hat{L}^{t+k}$=RAS adjusted occupation-industry coefficient matrix

A_{ij}^t =actual occupation-industry flow matrix for year t

A_{ij}^{t+k} =actual occupation-industry flow matrix for year $t+k$

$\hat{A}_{ij}^{t+k}$ =RAS adjusted occupation-industry flow matrix

$j=1, 2,...m$=proportion of employees with occupation i in industry

$j=1, 2,..., n$=total employment in industry j, and $i\neq j$

ESS=error sum of squares

WESS=weighted error sum of squares

WMESS=weighted mean error sum of squares

WRM ESS=weighted root mean error sum of squares

χ^2=aggregate chi-square (based on flows)

W=weights, being derived from the elements of

L_{ij}^t and L_{ij}^{t+k} (e.g. $W_{ij}=L_{ij}^{t+k}/\sum_i\sum_j L_{ij}^{t+k}$).

Now, suppose that the SAB hypothesis is not accepted, we check whether changes in the coefficients during t and $t+k$ can be approximated by the biproportionality rule. For this, we compare the corresponding values of the test-statistics associated with the two respective hypothesis. If the values of the test-statistics associated with the RAS turn out to be smaller than the corresponding values of the SAB, the inference would be that the RAS provides a closer approximation of the evolution of occupational coefficient.

In addition to these tests, we also present a frequency distribution of errors by size of the adjusted occupational coefficients. These errors (ρ) are derived as:

$$\rho = \frac{A_{ij}^{t+k} - \hat{A}_{ij}^{t+k}}{A_{ij}^{t+k}} \times 100 \ \forall_{ij} \qquad \ldots(7.7)$$

The distribution is obtained for both the positive and the negative errors. The dispersions of the underlying distribution of error are presented in terms of their standard deviation, skewness and kurtosis. A graphic representation of these distributions is also attempted.

The weights (w_{ij}s) are used to offset some of the effects of high inter-industry differences in their skill-mix; especially when the matrices are in the coefficient form. These weights are taken to be employment in each cell as a proportion of total employment in all the industries included in the sample.

THE DATA

This exercise is based on the data obtained from the unpublished reports of the Directorate General of Employment and Training (D.G.E. & T.) for a sample of manufacturing industries in public and private sectors cross-classified by 13 occupational categories. Since the necessary details about the definitions, coverage and the various limitations of these data have already been spelt out in Chapter 4, we shall not repeat them here. In view of the under-estimation in the coverage of industry-wise employment, a pro rata adjustment on the lines suggested in Chapter 4 is applied.

As already stated, this exercise is carried out separately for the private and the public sectors.[7] The construction of occupation-industry matrices for these sectors is described below.

Let us first describe the private sector. Given the matrix for 1963, and row and column total for 1967 and 1971, respectively, the RAS adjusted matrix is obtained for 1967 and 1971. A sample of 49 industries in the private sector is considered for the adjustment with their employment profile broken down into 13 occupations. These occupations are as under:

1. (00) Architects, engineers, surveyors, etc.
2. (01) Chemists, physicists, geologists and other physical scientists.
3. (02-08) Biologists, agronomists, physicians, surgeons, nurses, teachers, artists, jurists, writers, etc.
4. (09-0X) Draughtsmen, science and engineering technicians and other professional, technical and related workers.
5. (Div. 1) Administrative, executive and managerial workers.
6. (Div. 2) Clerical and related workers.
7. (Div. 3) Sales workers.
8. (Div. 4) Farmers, fishermen, hunters, loggers, etc.
9. (Div. 5) Miners, quarrymen and related workers.
10. (Div. 6) Workers in transport and communication occupations.
11. (Div. 7) Craftsmen, process workers and labourers (n.e.c.).
12. (Div. 8) Craftsmen, production process workers and labourers (n.e.c.).
13. (Div. 9) Sports and recreation workers.

With the row and column total for two different periods (i.e. 1967 and 1971), an attempt is made to evaluate the usefulness of this method for short and medium term forecasting.

Now, we turn to the public sector. Given the base year matrix for 1964, and the row and column totals for 1972, the

RAS adjusted matrix is worked out for 28 public sector manufacturing establishments for 1972. The occupational classification follows that for the private sector.

Some comments regarding our choice of the occupations and industries are in order. As shown above, altogether 13 occupations are considered and these occupations are common in both the sectors. The choice of these occupations was guided by information content consideration as spelt out in Chapter 4 of the present study.

The sample of industries differs between public and private sectors (i.e., 49 in private sector and 28 in public sector). This is primarily because we do not include industries which exhibit a highly erratic growth pattern in the share of certain occupations during the base and the terminal years.

Since the sample of industries for this exercise includes only those establishments which are listed in Appendix 4.1, we do not mention them again. Only industry codes are stated when necessary.

THE RESULTS

Private sector

Given the base year matrix for 1963, and row and column totals for 1967 and 1971, respectively, the RAS adjustments are carried out for 4 and 8 years' intervals. As already mentioned, the alternative time spans are considered to check whether the adjustments for different time periods are uniformly reliable.

The two RAS adjusted matrices (i.e., for 1967 and 1971) are presented in Tables 7.2 and 7.3. With some exceptions, most of the adjusted coefficients seem plausible. The clerical workers (Div. 2) and the sports and recreation workers (Div. 9) are somewhat inflated in a few industries. For instance, the coefficient of clerical workers in water-proof textile products (SIC. 275) is as high as .38 (Table 7.2). Other industries for which the coefficient of clerical workers is high are edible fat and oil (SIC. 207), vanaspati (SIC. 208), production of petroleum, kerosene, etc. (SIC. 324) and soap and other

TABLE 7.2: **RAS adjusted occupation-industry coefficient matrix—private sector: 1967**

Sl. No.	Industry Codes (SIC) / Occupations (NCO)	200	201	202	203	205	206	207
1	00	.0006	.0241	.0041	.0047	.0078	.0082	.0186
2	01	.0002	.0127	.0004	.0098	.0036	.0078	.0109
3	02-08	.0021	.0267	.0025	.0050	.0031	.0140	.0172
4	09-0X	.0001	.0083	.0020	.0005	.0022	.0209	.0087
5	Div. 1	.0109	.0100	.0082	.0103	.0159	.0281	.0390
6	Div. 2	.0406	.1436	.0431	.0754	.1353	.1792	.2684
7	Div. 3	.0008	.0012	.0007	.0109	.0204	.1068	.0142
8	Div. 4	.0028	.0330	.4898	.0018	.0019	.1154	.0030
9	Div. 5	.0003	.0005	—	—	.0006	—	.0003
10	Div. 6	.0022	.0214	.0046	.0102	.0188	.0355	.0218
11	Div. 7	.0160	.1875	.0260	.3933	.0454	.0446	.2000
12	Div. 8	.9019	.4279	.3941	.4761	.7171	.4037	.3876
13	Div. 9	.0215	.1031	.0245	.0020	.0278	.0358	.0103

TABLE 7.2: (*Contd.*)

Sl. No.	Industry Codes (SIC) / Occupations (NCO)	208	209	217	230	239	241	270
1	00	.0305	.0019	.0002	.0084	.0016	.0070	.0001
2	01	.0363	.0009	—	.0006	.0005	.0001	—
3	02-08	.0164	.0019	.0043	.0064	.0066	.0024	.0006
4	09-0X	.0248	.0004	—	.0003	.0016	.0002	.0012
5	Div. 1	.0249	.0262	.0148	.0213	.0125	.0029	.0011
6	Div. 2	.2532	.0496	.0501	.0554	.0728	.0425	.0065
7	Div. 3	.0327	.0076	.0098	.0009	.0019	.0001	.0009
8	Div. 4	.0062	.0034	.0097	.0012	.0020	.0029	.0018
9	Div. 5	—	—	—	.0004	—	.0003	.0007
10	Div. 6	.0187	.0062	.0079	.0027	.0047	.0018	.0098
11	Div. 7	.2449	.0230	.0852	.3275	.6827	.6817	.7690
12	Div. 8	.3043	.7809	.8152	.5123	.1160	.2219	.1738
13	Div. 9	.0071	.0980	.0028	.0626	.0971	.0362	.0344

TABLE 7.2: (*Contd.*)

Sl. No.	Industry Codes (SIC) / Occupations (NCO)	271	273	275	281	292	310	311
1	00	.0015	.0018	.0242	.0011	.0018	.0023	.0176
2	01	—	.0245	—	.0038	.0004	.0005	.0002
3	02-08	.0049	.0065	.0152	.0065	.0059	.0026	.0034
4	09-0X	.0002	.0012	—	.0007	.0036	.0003	.0052
5	Div. 1	.0258	.0079	.0084	.0191	.0152	.0181	.0163
6	Div. 2	.0922	.0728	.3820	.0926	.1032	.0562	.0969
7	Div. 3	.0026	.0060	.0042	.0011	.0022	.0014	.0005
8	Div. 4	.0006	.0015	.0044	.0005	.0449	.0020	.0005
9	Div. 5	—	—	—	—	—	—	—
10	Div. 6	.0031	.0047	.0096	.0088	.0091	.0036	.0030
11	Div. 7	.7356	.7524	.1868	.6866	.0293	.0762	.6063
12	Div. 8	.0763	.0289	.3042	.1387	.7582	.7952	.2371
13	Div. 9	.0572	.0918	.0610	.0405	.0262	.0416	.0130

TABLE 7.2: (*Contd.*)

Sl. No.	Industry Codes (SIC) / Occupations (NCO)	320	324	330	331	332	333	335
1	00	.0981	.0428	.0439	.0228	.0396	.0179	.0131
2	01	.0011	.0125	.0185	.0450	.0209	.0011	·0360
3	02-08	.0132	.0142	.0121	·0061	.0088	.0049	.0227
4	09-0X	.0071	.0076	.0129	.0142	.0124	.0095	.0140
5	Div. 1	.0231	.0286	.0129	.0198	.0168	.0136	.0195
6	Div. 2	.1823	.2346	.1486	.1726	.0874	.0540	.1653
7	Div. 3	.0049	.0223	.0065	.0125	.0014	.0012	.0538
8	Div. 4	.0044	.0013	.0022	.0043	.0031	.0006	.0042
9	Div. 5	.0014	.0089	.0010	—	.0012	—	—
10	Div. 6	.0163	.0262	.0246	.0110	.0358	.0079	.0093
11	Div. 7	.0948	.1743	.1554	.1437	.1224	.0910	·0356
12	Div. 8	.5104	.3429	.4947	.4956	.5817	.7393	.5938
13	Div. 9	.0429	·0338	.0657	.0524	.0685	.0589	.0327

TABLE 7.2: (*Contd.*)

Sl. No.	Industry Codes (SIC) / Occupations (NCO)	336	341	347	351	357	359	360
1	00	.0109	.0196	.0006	.0025	.0069	.0292	.0310
2	01	.0103	.0053	.0022	.0006	.0014	.0011	.0031
3	02-08	.0098	.0162	.0017	.0037	.0044	.0077	.0211
4	09-0X	.0029	.0102	.0019	.0018	.0025	.0071	.0079
5	Div. 1	.0300	.0161	.0076	.0093	.0077	.0092	.0109
6	Div. 2	.2300	.1485	.0809	.0583	.0584	.1286	.1108
7	Div. 3	.0825	.0014	.0016	.0018	.0013	.0076	.0003
8	Div. 4	.0027	.0032	.0008	.0063	.0017	.0053	.0015
9	Div. 5	—	.0113	.0124	.0007	.0010	.0004	.0005
10	Div. 6	.0152	.0195	.0064	.0024	.0090	.0069	.0189
11	Div. 7	.0831	.1830	.3024	.0579	.0882	.1534	.3047
12	Div. 8	.4821	.5181	.5607	.8371	.7902	.6185	.4553
13	Div. 9	.0404	.0476	.0208	.0176	.0273	.0250	.0340

TABLE 7.2: (*Contd.*)

Sl. No.	Industry Codes (SIC) / Occupations (NCO)	361	363	368	370	371	372	374
1	00	.0101	.0148	.0134	.0259	.0752	.0357	.0552
2	01	.0029	.0032	.0026	.0003	.0004	.0002	.0001
3	02-08	.0137	.0072	.0059	.0068	.0040	.0055	.0064
4	09-0X	.0069	.0118	.0039	.0091	.0140	.0099	.0204
5	Div. 1	.0085	.0163	.0128	.0002	.0149	.0170	.0153
6	Div. 2	.0785	.1072	.0922	.0755	.1190	.0873	.1526
7	Div. 3	.0027	.0025	.0027	.0010	.0016	.0018	.0013
8	Div. 4	.0008	.0041	.0013	.0011	.0029	.0034	.0021
9	Div. 5	.0020	.0004	.0005	.0033	.0006	.0002	.0004
10	Div. 6	.0092	.0085	.0059	.0045	.0044	.0050	.0106
11	Div. 7	.4333	.4966	.3884	.7070	.4710	.6023	.5158
12	Div. 8	.3758	.2733	.4284	.1467	.2620	.2020	.1845
13	Div. 9	.0556	.0541	.0420	.0186	.0300	.0297	.0353

TABLE 7.2: (*Contd.*)

Sl. No.	Industry Codes (SIC) / Occupations (NCO)	375	376	377	382	386	391	395
1	00	.0200	.0424	.0085	.0511	.0278	.0281	.0074
2	01	.0003	.0004	.0046	.0017	.0012	.0018	.0018
3	02-08	.0060	.0090	.0053	.0058	.0082	.0068	.0060
4	09-0X	.0032	.0062	.0148	.0082	.0173	.0114	.0015
5	Div. 1	.0121	.0137	.0345	.0142	.0086	.0116	.0175
6	Div. 2	.0964	.1346	.1479	.1119	.1323	.0798	.1192
7	Div. 3	.0035	.0017	.0159	.0013	.0008	.0046	.0045
8	Div. 4	.0032	.0074	.0058	.0010	.0010	.0044	.0010
9	Div. 5	—	.0002	.0020	—	.0005	.0006	.0008
10	Div. 6	.0047	.0100	.0180	.0234	.1672	.0043	.0057
11	Div. 7	.3756	.3574	.3556	.4894	.3193	.5786	.1488
12	Div. 8	.4435	.3530	.3462	.2450	.2554	.2330	.6472
13	Div. 9	.0315	.0640	.0409	.0470	.0604	.0350	.0386

washing compounds (SIC. 336). At the other extreme is the coefficient for manufacture of carpet and other textile products (SIC. 270) which is as low as .006.

The share of sports and recreation workers after adjustment is somewhat high in certain food and cotton textile industries. For example, we observe from Table 7.2 that the adjusted coefficients of this occupational category in industries producing sugar and syrup (SIC. 201), food products (SIC. 209), cotton, cordage, rope, twine (SIC. 239), etc., turn out to be around .100. It implies that 10 per cent of the total employment of these industries consisted of sports and recreation workers. Similar instances or over-estimation may also be found for some other skills, such as sales workers (SIC. 206), farmers and fishermen (SIC. 202), etc.

The adjusted occupation-industry matrix for 1971 is presented in Table 7.3. We observe that the adjusted coefficients of this matrix exhibit a similar pattern as we find in 1967. In particular, the implausible cells of the 1967 matrix remain implausible in 1971 as well. This might be the consequence of (a) the common base year for both the adjustments (notice that the base year for both the adjustments is 1963), and (b) the even spreading of changes in the RAS. If the base year skill coefficients are high (or low) for certain industries, the proportionality rule of RAS method is likely to over- (or under-) estimate them. This suggests an important limitation of the RAS.

The real problem with the $\hat{r}$ and $\hat{s}^*$ multipliers relates to their interpretation. While in the input-output framework, these multipliers are usually interpreted as the 'substitution' and the 'fabrication' effects, respectively, an analogous interpretation of $\hat{r}$ and $\hat{s}^*$ in the present context might not be justifiable. For example, unless there is reason to believe that an increase or a decrease in skill coefficients is determined mainly by their relative prices and also that these prices have an identical impact across the sample of industries, it is not self-evident that $\hat{r}$ represents the substitution effect.

TABLE 7.3: **RAS adjusted occupation-industry coefficient matrix—private sector: 1971**

Sl. No.	Industry Codes (SIC) / Occupations (NCO)	200	201	202	203	205	206	207
1	00	.0006	.0234	.0034	.0046	.0078	.0079	.0184
2	01	.0002	.0103	.0003	.0080	.0030	.0062	.0090
3	02-08	.0023	.0270	.0022	.0050	.0033	.0139	.0178
4	09-0X	.0001	.0077	.0016	.0004	.0022	.0187	.0081
5	Div. 1	.0149	.0134	.0094	.0138	.0220	.0370	.0532
6	Div. 2	.0364	.1251	.0321	.0662	.1217	.1534	.2386
7	Div. 3	.0008	.0010	.0006	.0106	.0203	.1012	.0139
8	Div. 4	.0039	.0453	.5737	.0025	.0026	.1555	.0042
9	Div. 5	.0016	.0025	.0017	—	.0010	—	.0060
10	Div. 6	.0025	.0244	.0044	.0117	.0221	.0398	.0255
11	Div. 7	.0171	.1950	.0230	.4120	.0487	.0455	.2124
12	Div. 8	.8955	.4128	.3248	.4628	.7140	.3827	.3815
13	Div. 9	.0241	.1121	.0228	.0024	.0313	.0382	.0114

TABLE 7.3: (*Contd.*)

Sl. No.	Industry Codes (SIC) / Occupations (NCO)	320	324	330	331	332	333	335
1	00	.0974	.0410	.0435	.0228	.0389	.0178	.0132
2	01	.0009	.0099	.0153	.0375	.0171	.0009	.0302
3	02-08	.0137	.0141	.0125	.0063	.0090	.0050	.0239
4	09·0X	.0066	.0068	.0119	.0134	.0114	.0089	.0133
5	Div. 1	.0316	.0377	.0176	.0273	.0225	.0186	.0272
6	Div. 2	.1622	.2016	.1318	.1551	.0770	.0480	.1497
7	Div. 3	.0048	.0212	.0064	-0125	.0014	.0011	.0540
8	Div. 4	.0061	.0017	.0031	.0061	.0043	.0009	.0060
9	Div. 5	.0071	.0421	.0049	—	.0059	—	.0001
10	Div. 6	.0190	.0295	.0286	.0130	.0414	.0092	.0111
11	Div. 7	.1006	.1786	.1656	.1541	.1286	.0966	.0385
12	Div. 8	.5024	.3260	.4860	.4931	.5671	.7276	.5959
13	Div. 9	.0476	.0899	.0728	.0588	.0754	.0654	.0369

TABLE 7.3: (*Contd.*)

Sl. No.	Industry Codes (SIC) / Occupations (NCO)	336	341	347	351	357	359	360
1	00	.0109	.0186	.0006	.0025	.0068	.0292	.0304
2	01	.0086	.0042	.0017	.0005	.0011	.0009	.0026
3	02-08	.0102	.0160	.0017	.0039	.0046	.0079	.0215
4	09-0X	.0027	.0091	.0018	.0017	.0022	.0067	.0073
5	Div. 1	.0415	.0211	.0102	.0128	.0106	.0126	.0147
6	Div. 2	.2069	.1264	.0702	.0523	.0520	.1148	.0974
7	Div. 3	.0822	.0013	.0015	.0018	.0013	.0075	.0003
8	Div. 4	.0039	.0043	.0011	.0088	.0024	.0075	.0021
9	Div. 5	—	.0527	.0280	—	.0052	.0017	.0024
10	Div. 6	.0179	.0218	.0073	.0028	.0105	.0081	.0218
11	Div. 7	.0894	.1859	.3138	.0619	.0938	.1635	.3195
12	Div. 8	.4804	.4881	.5396	.8313	.7792	.6116	.4429
13	Div. 9	.0454	.0505	.0225	.0197	.0303	.0280	.0371

TABLE 7.3: (*Contd.*)

Sl. No.	Industry Codes (SIC) / Occupations (NCO)	361	363	368	370	371	372	374
1	00	.0095	.0141	.0131	.0249	.0732	.0343	.0536
2	01	.0023	.0026	.0021	.0002	.0003	.0002	.0001
3	02-08	.0133	.0073	.0060	.0068	.0038	.0055	.0065
4	09-0X	.0060	.0107	.0036	.0082	.0128	.0089	.0185
5	Div. 1	.0110	.0216	.0171	.0002	.0200	.0224	.0204
6	Div. 2	.0657	.0926	.0807	.0650	.1034	.0750	.1325
7	Div. 3	.0025	.0024	.0026	.0010	.0016	.0017	.0012
8	Div. 4	.0010	.0055	.0017	.0016	.0039	.0046	.0029
9	Div. 5	.0387	.0020	—	.0003	.0029	.0012	.0018
10	Div. 6	.0101	.0097	.0067	.0051	.0050	.0056	.0121
11	Div. 7	.4332	.5119	.4055	.7269	.4885	.6170	.5347
12	Div. 8	.3486	.2613	.4151	,1400	.2521	.1918	.1775
13	Div. 9	.0581	.0583	.0458	.0198	.0325	.0318	.0382

TABLE 7.3: (*Contd.*)

Sl. No.	Industry Codes (SIC) / Occupations (NCO)	375	376	377	382	386	391	395
1	00	.0196	.0413	.0088	.0489	.0258	0270	.0073
2	01	.0002	.0003	.0037	.0013	.0009	.0015	.0015
3	02-08	.0060	.0091	.0053	.0057	.0078	.0067	.0063
4	09-0X	.0029	.0056	.0134	.0074	.0149	.0103	.0014
5	Div. 1	.0163	.0184	.0458	.0087	.0110	.0153	.0239
6	Div. 2	.0844	.1175	.1280	.0960	.1093	.0686	.1064
7	Div. 3	.0034	.0016	.0153	.0014	.0003	.0043	.0044
8	Div. 4	.0044	.0101	.0071	.0014	.0013	.0061	.0014
9	Div. 5	—	.0011	.0096	.0083	.0370	.0027	—
10	Div. 6	.0055	.0115	.0205	.0263	.1812	.0048	.0068
11	Div. 7	.3927	.3724	.3671	.5014	.3147	.5935	.1584
12	Div. 8	.4301	.3414	.3315	.2328	.2336	.2217	.6393
13	Div. 9	.0345	.0697	.0439	.0504	.0622	.0375	.0429

Let us now describe the results of the test-statistics which have been used to check whether or not the occupational coefficients remain constant over time (i.e., the SAB hypothesis). Table 7.4 presents these results. This table suggests a very high inter-temporal variation in skill coefficients. For example, over a period of 4 years, i.e., between 1963 and 1967, the variation in coefficients, measured in terms of error sum of squares (ESS), turns out to be as high as 75.3. This value is, however, slightly decreased (i.e., from 75.3 to 68.9) when the variations are measured with a longer time span, i.e., over 1963 and 1971. The over time variability of skill coefficients is also confirmed by the other test measures (see Table 7.4). It would, therefore, be naive to assume that the base year occupation-industry coefficient matrix will remain unchanged over the period of projections.

Let us now turn to the RAS hypothesis. Several criteria of goodness of fit are considered.[8] The strategy here is to compare the RAS adjustment with no adjustment at all (i.e., SAB) in terms of the criteria in question. If the values of the test-statistics associated with the RAS turn out to be smaller than the corresponding values of the SAB, the inference would be that the RAS provides a closer approximation to changes in the occupational coefficients.

It appears from Table 7.4 that the goodness of results of the RAS adjusted matrices is quite satisfactory. The test-statistics associated with the RAS adjustment yield smaller values in relation to those with the SAB. For instance, the aggregated χ^2 shows a reduction of 79.5 per cent when the RAS adjustment is applied to 1963 occupation-industry matrix with the row and column totals for 1967. The error, however, increases when the period of adjustment is extended from 4 to 8 years. Using the same test criterion, Table 7.4 shows that the χ^2 value increases from 7.93 lakhs for 1967 to 17.15 lakhs for 1971. It may, therefore, be inferred that the method in question is more appropriate for short-term forecasting.

In addition to the χ^2, the other test measures also confirm this result. For example, the error sum of squares is reduced from 75.3 for the SAB to 1.6 for the RAS adjusted matrix of 1967. This shows that the value of ESS is reduced after

TABLE 7.4: **Goodness of fit of RAS adjustment: 1967 and 1971 (private sector)**

Test Statistics	1967			1971		
	SAB	RAS	RAS/SAB	SAB	RAS	RAS/SAB
ESS	75.26420	1.62813	0.02163	68.95041	2.26120	0.03279
WESS	2.21061	0.00467	0.00211	1.49086	0.00628	0.00421
WESS/ESS	0.02937	0.00287	—	0.02162	0.00278	—
WMESS	0.00347	0.00007	0.00202	0.00234	0.00001	0.00427
WRMESS	0.05891	0.00271	0.04600	0.04838	0.00314	0.06490
χ^2 (in lakhs)	38.68	7.93	0.20501	43.66	17.15	0.39281

the underlying adjustment by well over 97 per cent. When the period of adjustment is extended to 1971, the reduction in the value of ESS is 96.7 per cent. The reduction in the error seems to be smaller for longer periods of adjustment.

Since both adjusted and actual matrices are in the coefficient form, the weighted error sum of squares (WESS) was also computed. (The weights are taken to be employment in each cell as a proportion of total employment in the sample of industries). Comparing the WESS obtained from the adjusted and the actual matrices for 1963 and 1967, we note from Table 7.4 that the former is only 0.21 per cent of the latter. Similar results are obtained by comparing the RAS adjusted matrix for 1971 and the actual matrix for 1971 on the one hand, and the observed matrices for 1963 and 1971 for the SAB hypothesis on the other. The considerable reduction in the test-statistics suggests that the biproportional hypothesis provides a close approximation to the evaluation of occupational coefficients.

The more interesting results relate to the distribution of errors by size of occupational coefficients. Tables 7.5 and 7.6 present these distributions for 1967 and 1971, respectively. These tables are further arranged into A and B to present respectively the negative and the positive errors in the adjusted matrices.[9]

Three points may be noted from these tables. First, there does not seem to be a strong positive correlation between the size of a cell (i.e., occupational coefficient) and the error associated with that cell. In other words, it does not seem to be the case that the larger the cell the greater would be the error.

Second, the occupational coefficients ranging between 0 to 10 per cent (and, in some cases, 10 to 20 per cent) suffer from more frequent errors. There is, thus, an inverse relationship between the frequency of errors and the size of occupational coefficients.

Third, the magnitude of errors associated with smaller coefficients, in particular the coefficients which are below 10 per cent in size, are relatively higher than those of the larger coefficients. For example, we observe from Table 7.5-A that

TABLE 7.5-A: **Distribution of negative errors by size of occupational coefficients for 1967**

Negative error interval (%)	Size of occupational coefficients (%)									
	0-10	10-20	20-30	30-40	40-50	50-60	60-70	70-80	80-90	90-100
0-10	41	4	—	2	3	3	3	2	2	—
10-20	29	3	2	—	—	1	2	—	—	—
20-30	20	7	—	1	—	2	—	—	—	—
30-40	19	1	1	1	—	1	—	—	—	—
40-50	22	2	1	—	—	—	—	—	—	—
50-60	17	1	1	—	—	—	—	—	—	—
60-70	8	—	—	—	—	—	—	—	—	—
70-80	11	1	1	—	—	—	—	—	—	—
80-90	4	1	—	—	—	—	—	—	—	—
90-100	3	—	—	—	—	—	—	—	—	—
100 and above	63	1	—	—	—	—	—	—	—	—

TABLE 7.5-B: **Distribution of positive errors by size of occupational coefficients for 1967**

Positive error interval (%)	Size of occupational coefficients (%)									
	0-10	10-20	20-30	30-40	40-50	50-60	60-70	70-80	80-90	90-100
0-10	28	9	1	1	—	5	3	1	2	—
10-20	49	2	—	—	4	5	—	—	1	—
20-30	35	3	—	—	1	—	—	—	—	—
30-40	33	4	—	—	3	—	—	1	—	—
40-50	27	2	1	1	—	—	1	—	—	—
50-60	24	1	—	—	—	—	—	—	—	—
60-70	15	—	—	—	—	—	—	—	—	—
70-80	20	3	1	—	—	1	—	—	—	—
80-90	20	1	—	—	—	—	—	—	—	—
90-100	14	1	—	—	—	—	—	—	—	—

Mean error = (—) 1.727
Standard deviation = 53.668
Skewness = (—) 0.373
Kurtosis = (—) 0.494

TABLE 7.6-A : **Distribution of negative errors by size of occupational coefficients for 1971**

Negative error interval (%)	Size of occupational coefficients (%)									
	0-10	10-20	20-30	30-40	40-50	50-60	60-70	70-80	80-90	90-100
0-10	5	—	—	—	—	—	—	—	—	—
10-20	3	1	—	—	—	—	—	—	—	—
20-30	11	—	—	—	—	—	—	—	—	—
30-40	7	1	1	—	—	—	—	—	—	—
40-50	18	—	1	—	—	—	—	—	—	—
50-60	17	—	—	—	—	1	—	—	—	—
60-70	18	2	1	1	—	—	—	—	—	—
70-80	18	1	—	—	1	1	3	—	—	—
80-90	24	6	—	2	—	1	—	—	—	—
90-100	34	2	—	2	—	6	3	2	2	—
100 and above	88	2	—	—	—	—	—	—	—	—

TABLE 7.6-B: **Distribution of positive errors by size of occupational coefficients for 1971**

Positive error intervals (%)	Size of occupational coefficients (%)									
	0-10	10-20	20-30	30-40	40-50	50-60	60-70	70-80	80-90	90-100
0-10	37	7	—	2	4	3	1	2	—	—
10-20	31	3	5	1	1	4	1	—	1	—
20-30	28	5	1	—	—	1	—	—	—	—
30-40	39	1	1	—	1	1	—	2	—	—
40-50	36	3	—	—	—	1	1	—	—	—
50-60	11	—	1	—	—	—	—	—	—	—
60-70	22	2	1	—	—	—	—	—	—	—
70-80	24	2	—	1	—	—	—	—	—	—
80-90	21	3	—	—	—	1	—	—	—	—
90-100	16	1	1	—	—	—	—	—	—	—

Mean error	=(—)15.275
Standard deviation	= 66.098
Skewness	=(—) 0.036
Kurtosis	=(—) 1.433

63 occupational coefficients with their size ranging between 0 to 10 per cent show (negative) errors greater than 100 per cent. Such coefficients are 88 when the period of adjustment is extended from 1967 to 1971 (Table 7.6-A). In contrast to this, the number of cells associated with the high magnitude of error is sharply reduced as we move to higher percentages of the occupational coefficients. A uniform pattern emerges from distribution of both the negative as well as the positive errors, and for both the years of adjustment, i.e., 1967 and 1971 (see Tables 7.5-A, B and 7.6-A, B). Thus, there seems to be lesser risk involved in projecting the occupational structure of employment at the aggregate levels.

The mean value of errors, shown in Tables 7.5-B and 7.6-B, suggests that the RAS adjustment is more relevant for the short-term forecasting of demand for various occupations. This value increases from (—)1.727 in 1967 to (—)15.275 in 1971. The minus sign implies over-estimation in the adjusted matrices. A somewhat high standard deviation (i.e., 53.7 for 1967 and 66.1 for 1971) is suggestive of a large dispersion of error around the mean.

A graphical representation of these distributions is presented in Figures 7.1 and 7.2. The vertical axis of these figures shows absolute frequencies of occupational coefficients. The magnitude of errors associated with these frequencies is presented on the horizontal axis. Both the figures suggest that the distribution is negatively skewed—coefficients of skewness being (—)0.373 for 1967 and (—)0.036 for 1971 and also have flat peaks. Flatness of the peak is also confirmed by negative values of kurtosis which were (—)0.494 for 1967 and (—)1.433 for 1971. Two points may be noted from these figures: (a) the frequency of negative errors, arising out of overestimation in the adjusted matrices, is higher, and (b) a large number of occupational coefficients show higher percentages of errors.

Public sector

We now present the results for the public sector. These results are based on 13 occupations and 28 manufacturing

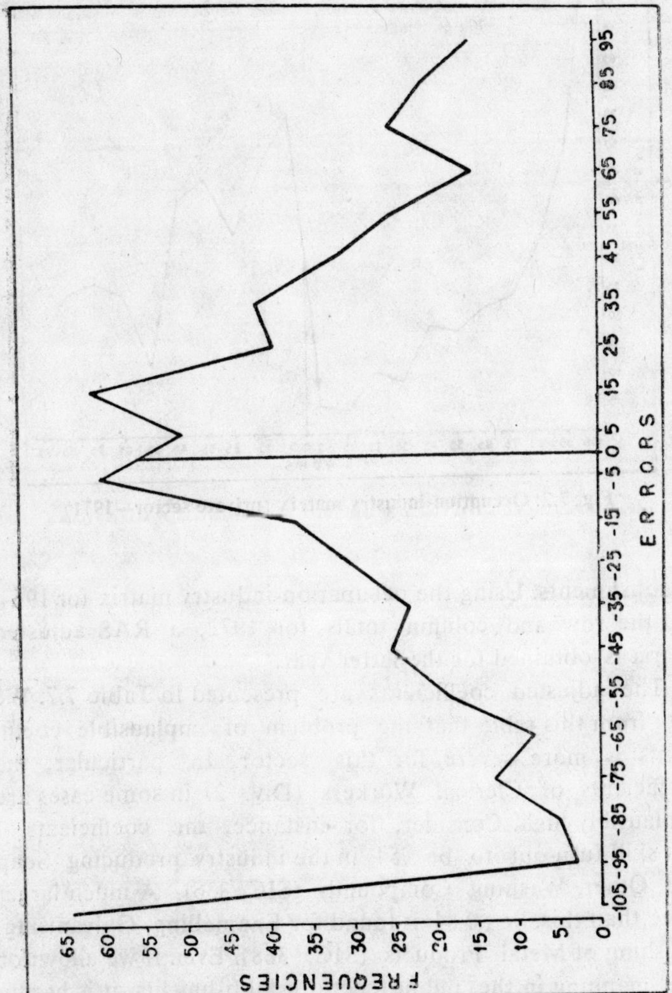

Fig. 7.1: Occupation-industry matrix (private sector —1967)

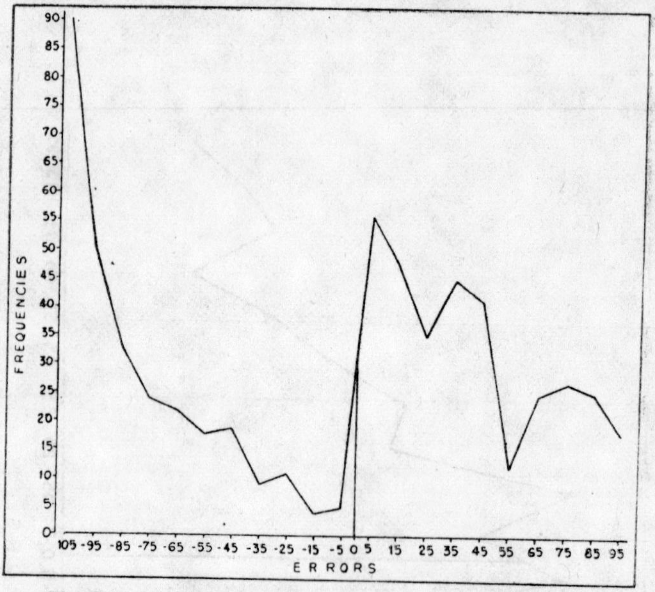

Fig. 7.2: Occuption-industry matrix (private sector—1971)

establishments. Using the occupation-industry matrix for 1964, and the row and column totals for 1972, a RAS adjusted matrix is obtained for the latter year.

The adjusted coefficients are presented in Table 7.7. We note from this table that the problem of implausible coefficients is more severe for this sector. In particular, the coefficients of Clerical Workers (Div. 2) in some cases are implausibly high. Consider, for instance, the coefficients of this skill turn out to be .54 in the industry producing Soap and Other Washing Compounds (SIC. 336). A much larger value than this, i.e., 0.84, is found for Enamelling, Galvanising, Polishing of Metal Products (SIC. 368). Even if we allow for over-manning in the public sector establishments, it is hardly conceivable that 84 per cent of the total employment in this industry would consist of Clerical Workers.

TABLE 7.7: **RAS adjusted occupation-industry coefficient matrix (public sector—1972)**

Sl. No.	Industry Codes (SIC) / Occupations (NCO)	201	206	271	273	281	311	320
1	00	.0030	.0025	.0671	.0001	.0038	.0139	.0041
2	01	.0020	.0011	.0273	.0001	.0010	.0022	.0016
3	02-08	.0050	.0151	.2208	.0037	.0201	.0035	.0027
4	09-0X	.0020	.0064	.0535	.0002	.0122	.0043	.0032
5	Div. 1	.0270	.0213	.0600	.0080	.0182	.0048	.0255
6	Div. 2	.1160	.1306	.0811	.0562	.1215	.0521	.1109
7	Div. 3	.0003	.1802	.0405	.0045	—	.0974	—
8	Div. 4	.0031	.0968	.0270	.0001	.0020	.0477	—
9	Div. 5	.0009	.0003	—	—	—	—	—
10	Div. 6	.0070	.0484	.0331	.0017	.0075	.0026	—
11	Div. 7	.0574	.0246	.0915	.7612	.7371	.0294	.0111
12	Div. 8	.7486	.3662	.0553	.1489	.0566	.6884	.7965
13	Div. 9	.0277	.1065	.2428	.0153	.0200	.0487	.0444

TABLE 7.7: (*Contd.*)

Sl. No.	Industry Codes (SIC) / Occupations (NCO)	324	330	332	333	335	336	341
1	00	.0791	.1434	.1408	.0035	.0370	.0150	.0045
2	01	.0043	.0034	.0066	.0362	.0453	.0976	.0024
3	02-08	.0555	.0403	.0351	.0086	.0353	.0395	.0310
4	09-0X	.0252	.0200	.0164	.0171	.0612	.0240	.0060
5	Div. 1	.0471	.0174	.0231	.0087	0365	.1074	.0181
6	Div. 2	.2869	.2660	.1315	.0270	.2331	.5449	.1176
7	Div. 3	.0064	.0006	.0012	.0016	.0006	.0181	.0004
8	Div. 4	.0044	.0045	.0045	0001	.0090	.0121	.0039
9	Div. 5	.0078	—	.0004	.0010	.0017	.0222	.0211
10	Div. 6	.1455	.0306	.0196	.0096	.0112	.0148	.0166
11	Div. 7	.0288	.2432	.2132	.1033	.1535	.0615	.1806
12	Div. 8	.1564	.1209	.3169	.7647	.2919	.0248	.5094
13	Div. 9	.1526	.1097	.0907	.0186	.0834	.0181	.0884

TABLE 7.7: (*Contd.*)

Sl. No.	Industry Codes (SIC) / Occupations (NCO)	351	357	359	360	368	370	371
1	00	.0149	.0088	.0221	.0236	.0083	.0989	.0138
2	01	.0005	.0006	.0019	.0017	.0017	.0002	.0002
3	02-08	.0051	.0011	.0145	.0308	.0027	.0456	.0131
4	09-0X	.0010	.0013	.0390	.0300	.0066	.0389	.0073
5	Div. 1	.0081	.0057	.0364	.0087	.0037	.0139	.0027
6	Div. 2	.0486	.0223	.1843	.1517	.8378	.1889	.1333
7	Div. 3	.0008	.0010	.C007	.0029	.0025	.0002	.0003
8	Div. 4	.0005	.0006	.C034	.0064	.0017	.0034	.0989
9	Div. 5	.0173	.0012	.C138	.0071	.0031	.0006	.0094
10	Div. 6	.0026	.0008	.0161	.0894	.0041	.0234	.0141
11	Div. 7	.0248	.2201	.1905	.3986	.1018	.3563	.4489
12	Div. 8	.8602	.7055	.4029	.1804	.0034	.1575	.1983
13	Div. 9	.0156	.0310	.0744	.0687	.0226	.0722	.0597

TABLE 7.7: (*Contd.*)

Sl. No.	Industry Codes (SIC) / Occupations (NCO)	372	374	375	376	382	386	391
1	00	.0270	.2775	.0202	.0222	.0007	.0378	.2686
2	01	.0001	.0002	.0003	.0002	—	.0001	.0003
3	02-08	.0220	.0525	.0028	.0185	.0037	.0096	.0161
4	09-0X	.0464	.0359	.0039	.0151	.0033	.0299	.0168
5	Div. 1	.0239	.0571	.0044	.0091	.0037	.0057	.0182
6	Div. 2	.1035	.3414	.1194	.1428	.0589	.0701	.1268
7	Div. 3	.0007	.0022	.0004	.0006	.0008	.0047	.0004
8	Div. 4	.0134	.0012	.0003	.0008	.0011	.0002	.0014
9	Div. 5	.0133	.0005	.0005	—	.0052	.0002	.0005
10	Div. 6	.0116	.0075	.0041	.0171	.0082	.0206	.0094
11	Div. 7	.5592	.1801	.6304	.1583	.6974	.5610	.4130
12	Div. 8	.1469	.0201	.1864	.5294	.1893	.2186	.0884
13	Div. 9	.0320	.0238	.0269	.0859	.0277	.0415	.0401

Some other occupations which seem to yield implausibly high or low coefficients after adjustment are the Sports and Recreation Workers (Div. 9), Managerial Workers (Div. 1), Sales Workers (Div. 3), etc. The adjusted coefficient of Sports and Recreation Workers in the Manufacture of Hosiery and Other Knitted Fabrics and Garments (SIC. 271) turns out to be 24. Similarly, the coefficient of Sales Workers in industry producing Butter, Ghee, Cheese and Other Dairy Products (SIC. 206) is rather high. It is somewhat doubtful that around one-fifth of the total work-force in this industry would belong to sales occupation. In contrast to these is the coefficient of Managerial Worker in the Manufacture of Shoes and Other Leather Footwear (SIC. 311). It turns out to be as low as 0.005 (Table 7.7). These examples further illustrate the limitation of the biproportional adjustment rule.

Despite a few implausible coefficients in Table 7.7, the results of the test-statistics used to evaluate the goodness of fit of the model are reassuring. These results are given in Table 7.8. This table shows that (a) the SAB hypothesis based on fixity in occupational coefficients over time may not be helpful for forecasting the structure of employment, and (b) the biproportional hypothesis of the RAS adjustment closely approximates the inter-temporal variation in occupational proportions of the sample of public sector manufacturing establishment. The basis of discarding the SAB hypothesis comes from the non-zero positive values of the test-statistics we have used. For instance, the error sum of squares (ESS), computed from the actual occupation-industry coefficient matrices for 1964 and 1972, turns out to be 725.4. This value is, however, reduced to 5.8 when the weights are applied[10] to account for some of the inter-industry variations in occupational coefficients. The mean and root mean of the weighted error sum of squares (WESS) are given as 0.016 and 0.126, respectively. The value of the aggregate χ^2 is as high as 268.5 lakhs. We do not, therefore, accept the SAB hypothesis as a basis of occupational forecasting.

Compared to SAB, the error is considerably low in the RAS adjusted matrix. Table 7.8, which suggests that the values of the test-statistics associated with the RAS are markedly lower than the corresponding values of the SAB, confirms this. We note from this table that the aggregate χ^2 obtained from the RAS adjusted matrix is only one-fourth of the SAB. It implies 75 per cent reduction in the value of the χ^2 on account of the biproportional adjustment of the RAS. The goodness of fit of RAS is also confirmed by ESS and WESS. While the ESS was 725.4 for the SAB, it turns out to be only 3.7 for the RAS. The weighted error sum of squares (WESS) of the two are 5.8 and 0.015, respectively. It follows, therefore, that the RAS yields a close approximation to the evolution of occupational coefficients.

TABLE 7.8: **Goodness of fit of RAS adjustment—1972 (Public sector)**

Test statistic	SAB	RAS	RAS/SAB
ESS	725.39847	3.74024	0.00516
WESS	5.80045	0.01472	0.00254
WESS/ESS	0.00800	0.00393	—
WMESS	0.01594	0.00004	0.00251
WRMESS	0.12623	0.00636	0.05038
χ^2 (in lakhs)	268.46	66.37	0.24722

The frequency distribution of errors by size of occupational coefficients is shown in Table 7.9. As in case of private sector, this table is broken down into 7.9-A and 7.9-B to represent the negative and the positive errors, respectively.

These tables confirm that the size of occupational coefficients and the frequency of errors are related inversely. Tables 7.9-A and 7.9-B show that the frequency of errors is not as high for the skills whose coefficients are above 10 per cent as for those which are below 10 per cent. Also, the size of errors associated with the latter is considerably large as compared to the former. We note, for example, from Table 7.9-A that as many as 60 cells of the first occupational decile (i.e., 0 to 10 per cent) have registered greater than 100 per cent (negative) errors. The number of cells with the same magnitude of error is, however, reduced to 3 as we move to the next occupational decile (i.e., 10 to 20 per cent). A similar trend may also be seen from Table 7.9-B.

TABLE 7.9-A: **Distribution of negative errors by size of occupational coefficients for 1972**

Negative error intervals (%)	Size of occupational coefficients (%)									
	0—10	10—20	20—30	30—40	40—50	50—60	60—70	70—80	80—90	90—100
0—10	3	1	—	1	—	—	—	—	—	—
10—20	5	—	—	—	—	—	—	—	—	—
20—30	4	1	—	—	—	—	—	—	—	—
30—40	3	—	—	—	—	1	—	—	—	—
40—50	7	1	—	—	2	—	—	—	—	—
50—60	3	1	1	—	1	—	—	—	—	—
60—70	9	3	—	—	—	—	—	—	—	—
70—80	7	1	—	—	1	—	—	—	—	—
80—90	6	2	2	2	2	—	—	—	—	—
90—100	14	4	—	—	—	—	—	—	—	—
100 and above	60	3	—	—	—	—	—	—	—	—

TABLE 7.9-B: **Distribution of positive errors by size of occupational coefficients for 1972**

Positive error intervals (%)	Size of occupational coefficients (%)									
	0—10	10—20	20—30	30—40	40—50	50—60	60—70	70—80	80—90	90—100
0—10	11	—	1	—	—	—	—	2	—	—
10—20	10	5	3	1	2	—	—	1	—	—
20—30	8	4	1	—	—	—	—	—	—	—
30—40	17	5	2	—	—	—	—	—	—	—
40—50	16	2	1	1	—	—	—	—	—	—
50—60	13	1	—	1	—	—	—	—	—	—
60—70	17	1	1	1	—	—	—	—	—	—
70—80	21	1	1	—	—	—	—	—	—	—
80—90	24	1	1	—	1	—	—	—	—	—
90—100	17	2	1	—	—	—	1	1	—	—

Mean error =(—) 4.031
Standard deviation= 72.357
Skewness =(—) 0.208
Kurtosis =(—) 1.505

Since the share of skills associated with larger magnitude of errors is mostly below 10 per cent of the total employment even large 'errors' may not imply large errors in projected employment at the aggregate level.

The mean and the standard deviation of errors are given as (−) 4.031 and 72.357, respectively, in Table 7.9-B. These values indicate overestimation in adjustment and a high dispersion of error around the mean, respectively. That the distribution is negatively skewed and platykurtic may be confirmed from the coefficients of skewness and kurtosis. The values of the respective coefficients are (−) 0.208 and (−) 1.505 (Table 7.9-B). The graphical representation of the underlying distribution is given in Figure 7.3.

CONCLUDING REMARKS

This chapter was mainly concerned with two competing hypotheses of changes in the occupational structure, viz., (*i*) the same as before hypothesis (SAB), and (*ii*) the RAS hypothesis. The same as before hypothesis premises that the occupational coefficients remain constant over time. The RAS hypothesis, on the other hand, is that the inter-temporal variations in industry-wise occupational coefficients are biproportional. These hypotheses were applied to Indian manufacturing industries data.

The criterion of the goodness of fit in this chapter reveals fairly large variations in industry-wise occupational coefficients over time. It, therefore, suggests that the SAB hypothesis as a basis for occupational forecasting would result in large errors.

The biproportionality rule of the RAS, on the other hand, provides a much close approximation to the evolution of the occupational structure(s). The test-statistics (e.g., the error sum of squares, the weighted error sum of squares, the weighted mean error sum of squares, the weighted root mean error sum of squares, the aggregate χ^2, etc.) favour the RAS.

The results of the test-statistics also indicate that the RAS adjustment may be more appropriate for short period forecasting (i.e., for 4-5 years). We note from our results that the

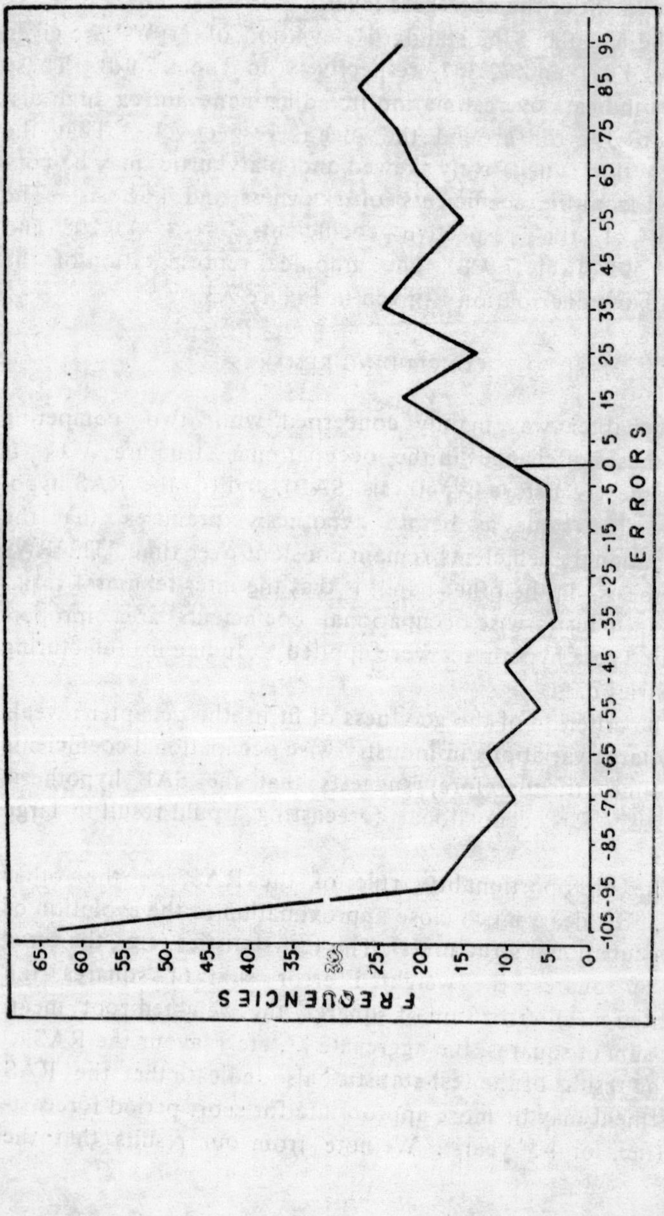

Fig. 7.3: Occupation-industry matrix (public sector—1972)

magnitude of errors increases when the period of adjustment is extended from 4 to 8 years (i.e., from 1963-1967 to 1963-1971).

The distribution of errors by size of occupational coefficients in the RAS adjusted occupation-industry matrices suggests an inverse relationship between the size of the coefficients and the frequency of error. In other words, the larger the coefficients the lower is the frequency and the magnitude of error. Hence, the errors in the forecasts in absolute terms may not, in general, be large.

We note from Figures 7.1, 7.2 and 7.3 that the distribution of errors is negatively skewed, i.e., the left tail is longer. This means that there are very large negative errors in the distribution. Since the mean error for most of the distributions in question is negative, it is likely that, in general, the RAS adjustment will tend to overestimate some coefficients.

Although the RAS emerges relatively unscathed as a method of projecting the occupational structure of employment, some limitations of this method ought not to be overlooked. One of these is the risk that, if the initial value of any particular coefficient is high, it is likely that the adjusted value would be an overestimate. Another limitation is that an exact biproportional hypothesis may be appropriate in only a few specific cases. A more flexible version of the RAS which admits of random variations around biproportional movements of the coefficients in question, is intuitively much more appealing. A third limitation is that while the RAS adjustment helps in reducing the errors in projections, a satisfactory explanation of the factors shaping the occupational structure still eludes us.

REFERENCES

1. An early application of this technique in manpower forecasting is due to a group of economists of the manpower forecsating unit at the University of Warwick [see, for example, Evans and Lindley (1972), Bosworth *et al* (1974), etc.]. This has subsequently been applied by Gaiha (1977) on the basis of occupational data obtained for a cross-section of manufacturing industries in India.
2. Bacharach (1970) has proved the convergence existence property of the RAS model and its uniqueness unconditionally. The bipropor-

tional relationship of the RAS method clearly preserves the zeros of the base year matrix A^t_{ij}. Moreover, the non-negativity of the forecast is an obvious *a priori* condition; if the number of zeros (null elements) are large or occur systematically over the entire row or column of the matrix, then suitable adjustment may be required. Since our occupation-industry matrices do not suffer from this problem, no such adjustments are made.

3. For a demonstration of this, see Lecomber (1969).
4. It is doubtful that this feature of the RAS adjustment can be justified in an inter-temporal context.
5. Since each test-statistic is a scaler measure of the deviation between the observed and the estimated coefficients, it may not be advisable to rely on any particular statistic.
6. Note that the χ^2 test is applied to the corresponding flow matrices. The null hypothesis for the χ^2 test is that the occupation-industry matrices (observed and adjusted) are similar.
7. A justification for separating out the establishments in the public and private sectors is given in Chapter 5 (Section 3) of this thesis.
8. Altogether five different measures are used to check for the goodness of fit. These are the error sum of squares (ESS), the weighted error sum of squares (WESS), the weighted mean error sum of squares (WMESS), the weighted root mean error sum of squares (WRMESS and the aggregate χ^2. For a detailed discussion on these test criteria, see Section 3 of this chapter.
9. Note that the negative errors (i.e., $\rho = \dfrac{A^{t+k}_{ij} - \hat{A}^{t+k}_{ij}}{A^{t+k}_{ij}} < 0$) in the present context suggest overestimation of *i*th skill in industry *j*. An opposite will, however, be true when the errors are positive (i.e., $\rho > 0$).
10. As already pointed out, the weights are taken to be the proportion of *i*th skill in industry *j* to the total employment in the observed sample of industries.

8

APPLICATION OF THE RAS ADJUSTMENT TO OCCUPATION-EDUCATION RELATIONSHIPS

THE MANPOWER forecasting approach to educational planning seeks to link educational expansion to manpower requirements. This requires projection of occupation-education relationships. Considering the simplicity and the relatively modest data requirements of the RAS method, an attempt is made in this chapter to examine its appropriateness for adjusting temporal variations in occupation-education matrices for the public sector establishments.

An important question that arises while constructing the occupation-education matrix is the stability of the occupation-wise educational coefficients. If these coefficients vary over time (e.g., due to changes in technological or scale factors) adjustment of these coefficients for likely changes over time would be necessary to ensure reliable forecasts. We report in this chapter the results of the RAS adjustment. While the inferences drawn from these results are tentative, as they relate to a very limited number of observations, they confirm that the RAS adjustment is to be preferred to the alternative 'same as before (SAB)' hypothesis.[1]

This chapter is divided into six sections. First, we shall state certain methodological issues in establishing a link between occupation and education. This is followed by a justification for deriving the requirements of educated manpower via occupation-education relationships at the sectoral/industrial level. Section three is devoted to the methodology. A detailed description of major data sources for constructing occupation-education matrices is presented in section four. Finally, a review of the statistical findings and some of the inferences drawn will be given.

LINK BETWEEN OCCUPATION AND EDUCATION

Usually, the demand for various categories of educated manpower is derived with an implicit assumption that the relationship between occupation and education does not vary between industries. Hence the observed occupation-education profile of workers is generally used at the aggregate level to forecast their future requirements. This implies:

(*i*) that the relationship between the two is stable with regard to changes in the industrial structure, and
(*ii*) that the observed occupation-education profile is in some sense optimal—i.e., it represents the minimum quantity of education which is essential for the performance of the task in question.

Let us examine these assumptions.

The notion on which the first assumption rests is that formal education imparts skills which are crucial for performance of major tasks in an occupation. Educational requirements are rigidly fixed for occupations such as lawyer, doctor, accountant, architect, engineer, etc. At the other extreme are the occupations, viz., manager, director, sales workers, clerks, etc. for which the educational requirements are not so rigidly fixed. Indeed, in these occupations the required skills may not have a great deal to do with formal education. Would, then, a reliance on formal educational requirements on the part of employers be at all rational? To understand this, a brief reference to the screening hypothesis would be helpful. This hypothesis is described below.

The screening hypothesis or the theory of credentialism is derived from the theory of decision making under uncertainty. Employers are usually forced to select newcomers without detailed information about their personality traits. Educational attainments which are believed to be correlated with certain desirable personality traits such as self-reliance, achievement-drive, etc. serve as a convenient sorting device.[2] Using education as a yardstick, the job seekers can easily be classified and ranked. Hence, even in relation to the class of occupations where the educational requirements are not so rigidly fixed, educational attainment might serve as a proxy for skills which employers value.[3]

Another assumption which is implicit in this approach is the notion of optimum educational requirements. Usually optimum educational requirements are interpreted as minimum educational requirements for performing a set of tasks. Blaug (1970) argues that this interpretation might not be appropriate in all situations. It is mentioned that different levels of education may be consistent with the 'requirements' of a task and often from observation it may not be easy to identify the minimum level of formal education. Let us consider this in detail.

Three different relationships between occupation and education are suggested:

(*i*) there is a minimum educational qualification for each occupation, below which the tasks in question cannot be carried out at all but above which additional qualifications have no economic value;

(*ii*) the output of workers in particular occupations increases with their educational qualifications, very gradually to begin with, then at a sharply increasing rate beyond a certain threshold levels, after which it levels off again; and

(*iii*) the productivity of workers in particular occupations increases monotonically with their educational qualifications, first at an increasing and then at a decreasing rate, but it never levels off.

These three cases are illustrated in Figure 8.1 [reproduced from Blaug (1370)] with educational qualification measured as a single dimension on the horizontal axis and productivity (or any other index of performance in the occupation) measured on the vertical axis. The three relationships mentioned above correspond to the three numbered curves. It is clear that the

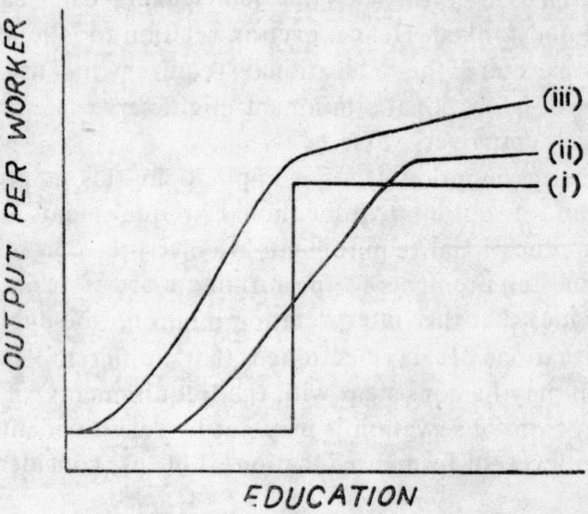

Fig. 8.1: Occupation-education relionships and productivity

first two relationships, marked (*i*) and (*ii*), respectively, are akin to the concept of minimum educational requirement. However, in case of (*iii*), the notion of minimum educational requirements cannot be defined independently of the relative costs of different categories of educated manpower. Let us take, for illustration, the price and productivity of two educational categories, say, graduate and matriculate. If the productivity of the former is twice as high as that of the latter, and if the price differential between the two is more than double, one would obviously prefer to employ the latter.

The relationship that holds in reality can only be conjectured in the absence of any firm empirical evidence. Another difficulty stems from the fact that work experience substitutes for formal education and training—especially among production process workers.[4] However, since we do not even have one complete set of occupation-education relationships (not even at the one-digit level of occupational classification cross-classified by industries) we hesitate to hazard a guess. Blaug's reservations about the notion of minimum educational requirements, which is implied in most manpower forecasts, are thus conjectural.

PROBLEMS OF FORECASTING THE OCCUPATION-EDUCATION RELATIONSHIPS

An important objective of forecasting the occupational structure is to relate the path of educational expansion to manpower needs of the economy. These two are usually related on the basis of given occupation-education relationships at the aggregate level. A reliance on a given aggregate occupation-education relationship would, however, imply that the evolution of the industrial structure over the projection period is not likely to be different from the trends in the past. This may or may not be true.

The next issue is the appropriateness of the observed occupation-education coefficients for forecasting purposes. One view is that, since these coefficients are the result of interaction of demand and supply at different points of time, they represent the evolution of the education system over a period of time. In a situation of labour market disequilibrium manifesting in a surplus of educated manpower, this possibility cannot be set aside. Another manifestation is the upgrading of minimum eligibility requirements for various occupational categories.[5] Admittedly, if the labour market has been in a state of disequilibrium certain distortions will be built into the forecasts. In fact, cases of engineering graduates working as technicians are often reported in newspapers. An opposite of it might also be the case. However, unless it could be established that substitutions of this kind are widespread, a reliance on the existing relationships would not be as hazardous as the critics of manpower forecasting suggest.

It should also be noted here that an aggregate occupational classification is somewhat risky in so far as intra-occupational shifts can cause changes in observed occupation-education relationships. The risk would be particularly great if the occupation-education relationships are set up at the aggregate level without allowing for differences in skill-mix ratios between public and private sectors. These differences might bring about intra-occupational shifts and thus alter the occupation-education relationships. An attempt is therefore made in this chapter to construct the sector and the industry specific occupation-education matrices at the two digit level of occupational classification. While it is true that even at this level of occupational disaggregation it is perhaps difficult to specify neatly the occupation-education relationships, a further disaggregation of occupations would have exceeded our resources.[6]

THE RAS ADJUSTMENT

The methodology

Let us first describe the model. Since a detailed description of the RAS formulation is given in Chapter 7 (Section 1), we shall be brief here.

This technique of adjusting the elements of a matrix from the given row and column totals is applied for computing shifts in occupation-wise structure of employment cross-classified by types and levels of education over time. This method assumes that changes in the elements of a matrix, Z_{ie}, through time are governed by 'row' effects and 'column' effects interacting multiplicatively. Two matrices in the series are then related by

$$\hat{Z}_{ie}^{t+k} = \hat{r}_i Z_{ie}^t \hat{s}_e \qquad \text{...(8.1)}$$

where Z_{ie} and $\hat{Z}_{ie}$ are the base and the adjusted occupation-education matrices $(m \times n)$ for years t and $t+k$, and $\hat{r}_i$ $(m \times m)$ and $\hat{s}_e$ $(n \times n)$ are the diagonal matrices of row and column multipliers, respectively. Each element of these matrices represents the number of workers with a given level of education.

Now suppose the Z^t_{ie} is known, and also the row and column totals for the terminal year $(t+k)$ so that

$$\hat{r}_i Z^t_{ie} s_e = \sum_e U^{t+k}_{ie} \qquad \ldots(8.2)$$

$$r'_i Z^t_{ie} \hat{s}_e = \sum_i V^{t+k}_{ie} \qquad \ldots(8.3)$$

where U is the column vector of the row sum of the updated (i.e., $\hat{Z}^{t+k}_{ie}$) flow matrix in year $t+k$, V is the row vector of its column sums, s is the column vector of the diagonal elements of $\hat{s}$, and r' is the column vector of the diagonal element of $\hat{r}$. The subscripts i $(i=1, 2, \ldots, m)$ and e $(e=1, 2, \ldots, n)$ denote occupation and education, respectively. The method involves a successive biproportional adjustment of the rows and columns of the base year matrix (Z^t_{ie}), until convergence is achieved.[7]

So far the adjustment procedure was described in relation to a flow matrix. If, instead of a flow matrix, the adjustment is needed to a given coefficient matrix subject to the row and column sum constraints, the method in question presents no difficulty as biproportional relationship between the flow matrices implies a biproportional relationship between the coefficient matrices.

Algebraically,

$$\hat{L}^{t+k}_{ie} = \hat{r}_i L^t_{ie} \hat{s}^*_e \qquad \ldots(8.4)$$

where L^t_{ie} and L^{t+k}_{ie} are the occupation-education coefficient matrices $(m \times n)$, and r $(m \times m)$ and s^* $(n \times n)$ are the diagonal matrices of the row and column multipliers, respectively. As mentioned earlier, the column multipliers, s^*, are different from the multipliers for the flow matrices. There is, however, a correspondence between the two sets of multipliers.[8] Since we are interested in adjusting coefficient matrices, it is the s^* which is relevant here.

Goodness of fit of the RAS adjustment

Following the criteria suggested in Chapter 7 (Section 2), the appropriateness of the two hypotheses [i.e., the same as before (SAB) and the RAS] are subjected to the following test-statistics:[9]

1. Error sum of squares (ESS).
2. Weighted error sum of squares (WESS)—weights are taken to be the proportionate share of *i*th occupation with *e*th education in the aggregate employment.
3. Weighted mean error sum of squares (WMESS).
4. Weighted root mean error sum of squares (WRMESS).
5. Aggregate Chi-Square (χ^2).

If the values of the test-statistics associated with the RAS are turned out to be smaller than the corresponding values of the SAB, we will infer that RAS provides a closer approximation of the over-time shifts in occupation-wise educational coefficients.

A frequency distribution of errors by size of educational coefficients is obtained for each of the adjusted matrices on the lines suggested in the previous chapter. Various measures of dispersion (e.g., standard deviation, skewness, kurtosis, etc.) have been used to assess the pattern of errors in the adjusted matrices.

An application of the concept of entropy is also carried out to describe the pattern of educational concentration in different occupations.[10]

THE DATA

A brief review of occupation-wise educational data is attempted below.

There are two important data sources on occupation-wise educational profile of workers in India. These are the decennial population censuses and the surveys conducted by the Directorate General of Employment and Training (DGE & T). Let us review the census data first.

The occupation-education profile of workers was presented for the first time in the 1961 census. It presents the educational data for occupations classified at the one digit level for urban areas only. As these data cover workers other than those engaged in cultivation, cultivators (both owners and tenants) and agricultural labourers are excluded from occupation division 4 (i.e., farmers, fishermen, hunters and loggers). The educational data on excluded categories are presented separately.

The educational classification especially at the university level is fairly detailed. At the school level a distinction is drawn between technical and general educations. At higher levels technical education is split into 7 categories, viz., (*i*) engineering, (*ii*) medicine, (*iii*) agriculture, (*iv*) veterinary and dairying, (*v*) technology, (*vi*) teaching, and (*vii*) others.

The second important source of occupation-education data is the DGE & T. It started collecting occupation-wise educational data in 1966. A difference between this and the census data is that the latter do not provide these relationships at the industry level. We have, therefore, relied on the DGE & T data to construct the occupation-education matrices. Some necessary details of these data are presented below.

The DGE & T provides education-wise data for professional and technical workers (Div. 0), Administrative, Executive and Managerial (Div. 1) and Craftsmen and Production Process Workers (Divs. 7 and 8). These data are collected at the five digit level of occupational classification, separately for the public and private sectors. In view of the difficulty of obtaining detailed educational data on an occupational basis from the private sector, the DGE & T decided to collect these data on a sample basis from private establishments employing 10 or more workers.[11] The public sector establishments are, however, covered on a complete enumeration basis.

Some of the problems which were faced in collecting these data are briefly described below. One problem was that there were a few groups of employees for which some employers reported all the prevalent but varied qualifications. In these cases, because a classification by eductional level was not feasible, it was assumed that all employees possessed the minimum qualification which was reported for the group as a whole. The other problem which might have resulted in more serious errors was the reporting of prescribed qualifications rather than the actual qualifications. Unfortunately, the exact number of such cases is not reported and hence it is difficult to make any adjustments to the data.

Another difficulty with the data arises out of non-comparability of the educational classifications over time, particularly between 1966 and 1972.[12] Since our occupation-education matrices relate to these two points of time, certain adjustments have been made to make the two classifications conformable. An adjusted educational profile of workers is as under:

1. Below Matric;
2. Matric and above (but below Graduate);
3. Graduate/Post-graduate/Ph. D. in Arts, Commerce, Law, etc;
4. Graduate/Post-graduate/Ph. D. in Science and Technology;
5. Degree in Professional subjects (including Certificate/ Diploma in Personnel Management or Business Administration);
6. Diploma in Science and Technology;
7. Certificate in Trade; and
8. Qualifications not available.

The first two educational categories were later combined as their individual shares turn out to be very low. Because it was not clear whether the last category (i.e., qualifications not available) consists of those without formal education, we have deleted it from the analysis.

Using these educational categories for four occupation divisions, aggregated at the two digit level, an attempt was made to capture temporal variations in occupation-education relationships in two public sector manufacturing industries. These industries are (*i*) Manufacture of Fertilizer (SIC. 332), and (*ii*) Manufacture of Machine Tools (SIC. 372). A list of the observed occupational groups (with their NCO codes) are as follows:

1. Architects, Engineers, Biologists, Agronomists, etc. (00+02);
2. Physicians, Surgeons and Dentists (03);
3. Nurses, Pharmacists and other Health Technicians (04);
4. Teachers (05);
5. Social Scientists and related Workers (07);
6. Draughtsmen, Science and Engineering Technicians (09);
7. Administrators and Executive Officials (10);
8. Directors, Managers, etc. (13);
9. Tailors, Cutters, etc. (71);
10. Furnacemen, Rollers, Drawers, etc. (73);
11. Toolmakers, Machinists, Plumbers, etc. (75);
12. Electricians and related Electronic Workers (76);
13. Carpenters, Joiners, Cabinet Makers (77); and
14. Compositors, Printers, etc. (80).

A similar exercise is attempted for professional and technical workers after taking all the public sector establishments together at the all-India level. Barring only few (e.g., engineers, chemists, meteorologists, geologists and agronomists), these workers were classified at the 5 digit level of occupational classification. The occupational titles and the NCO codes of these workers are given in Appendix 8.2.

It may be mentioned here that the adjustment is confined to the public sector because the educational details pertaining to this sector are obtained on a complete enumeration basis and hence the data would presumably be more reliable. The choice of industries is mainly guided by the size and distribution of employment. We have avoided industries with a large number of null cells.

DISCUSSION OF THE RAS ADJUSTMENT

We first present the results for professional and technical workers. Industry-wise analysis of educational profile of workers will follow subsequently.

Educational profile of professional and technical workers: Public sector

Using the base year matrix for 1966, and the row and column totals for 1972, the adjustment was derived for professional and technical workers in all the public sector establishments taken together at the all-India level. The adjusted coefficients for 1972 are presented in Table 8.1. This table shows that most of the coefficients are plausible. Also, there is some evidence of skill-specific concentration of education. Especially, the share of graduate or post-graduate workers is invariably large in most of those occupations which are education intensive. The coefficient of Graduate/Post-graduate in professional subjects, for example, is large for Civil Engineers (.90), Electrical Engineers (.78), Veterinary Surgeons (.97), Agronomists (.89), Physicians (.97), Surgeons (.98), etc. Similarly, the coefficient of Graduate/Post-graduate in Science is relatively large for such occupations as Chemists (.60), Meteorologists (.74), Science Teachers in Universities (.68), etc. (see Table 8.1).

The skill-specific concentration of education is further revealed by the adjusted values of entropies.[13] Since most of the entropies shown in Table 8.1 are close to zero, it implies that substantial proportions of workers are concentrated in particular educational categories.

The RAS provides that the closer approximation than the same as before (SAB) hypothesis can be seen from the values of the test statistics in Table 8.2. Comparing, for instance, the weighted error sum of squares (WESS) arising out of the SAB (i.e., the error which is likely to result if no adjustment is made to the actual matrix for 1966) and the RAS (i.e., the error likely to occur despite adjustment), we observe from this table that the latter is about 46 per cent of the former.

TABLE 8.1: **RAS adjusted occupation-education coefficient matrix: Professional and technical workers (public sector—1972)**

Occupations / Education	Engineers				Overseers	Chemist
	Civil	Mechanical	Electrical	Mining	Civil	
1. Below Matric	.0002	.0148	.0098	.0051	.0164	.0003
2. Matriculate and above (below Graduate)	.0134	.0816	.0728	.0327	.1489	.0427
3. Graduate/P.G., Ph. D. in Arts and Commerce	.0002	.0040	.0005	.1364	,0018	.0051
4. Graduate/P.G., Ph. D. in Science	.0053	.0884	.0106	.0247	.0059	.6001
5. Graduate/P.G., Ph. D. in Professional Subjects	.9023	.6854	.7777	.7309	.2030	.3442
6. Diploma Holders in Professional Subjects	.0786	.1258	.1286	.0702	.6240	.0076
Adjusted Entropies	.2100	.5714	.4163	.5121	.5640	.4876

TABLE 8.1: (*Contd.*)

Occupations / Education	Meteoro-logists	Geolo-gists	Veterin-ary Sur-geons	Agrono-mists	Physicians (General)	Surgeons (General)
1. Below Matric	.0000	.0007	.0002	.0009	.0001	.0000
2. Matriculate and above (below Graduate)	.0102	.0009	.0018	·0023	.0009	.0016
3. Graduate/P.G., Ph. D. in Arts and Commerce	.0121	.0104	.0022	.0013	.0010	.0019
4. Graduate/P.G., Ph. D. in Science	.7427	.2817	.0002	.0859	.0001	.0002
5. Graduate/P.G., Ph. D. in Professional Subjects	.2339	.7012	.9688	.8902	.9706	.9766
6. Diploma Holders in Professional Subjects	.0011	.0051	.0268	.0194	.0273	.0197
Adjusted Entropies	.3719	.3826	.0853	.2322	.0780	.0701

TABLE 8.1: (*Contd.*)

Occupations / Education	Physicians (Ayurvedic)	Health Officers	Nurses (General)	Midwives	Lady Health Visitors
1. Below Matric	.0002	.0004	.1800	.1852	.1974
2. Matriculate and above (below Graduate)	.0003	.0005	.1820	.0971	.5180
3. Graduate/P.G., Ph. D. in Arts and Commerce	.0003	.0006	.0024	.0067	.0350
4. Graduate/P.G., Ph. D. in Science	.0003	.0007	.0008	.0006	.0046
5. Graduate/P.G., Ph. D. in Professional Subjects	.7394	.9432	.0370	.0004	.0028
6. Diploma Holders in Professional Subjects	.2595	.0546	.5978	.7100	.2422
Adjusted Entropies	.3199	.1314	.5956	.4590	.6487

TABLE 8.1: (*Contd.*)

Occupations / Education	University teachers					Secondary school teachers		
	Arts	Science	Medicine and Surgery	Agriculture	Engineering	General	Arts (Drawing etc.)	Manual craft
1. Below Matric	.0000	.0000	.0000	.0000	.0000	.0075	.0426	.0386
2. Matriculate and above (below Graduate)	.0001	.0003	.0002	.0006	.0002	.0930	.2465	.2682
3. Graduate/P.G., Ph. D. in Arts and Commerce	.5308	.0694	.0002	.0007	.0109	.1041	.0885	.0278
4. Graduate/P.G., Ph. D. in Science	.0615	.6776	.0002	.2146	.0323	.0380	.0065	.0176
5. Graduate/P.G., Ph. D. in Professional Subjects	.3961	.2463	.9964	.7747	.8880	.7361	.0969	.0532
6. Diploma Holders in Professional Subjects	.0115	.0064	.0030	.0094	.0686	.0213	.5190	.5946
Adjusted Entropies	.5151	.4596	.0119	.3104	.2500	.5144	.7206	.6230

It suggests (a) that the occupation-wise educational coefficients vary over time (and hence, invalidates the SAB hypothesis), and (b) that around 54 per cent of the variations in educational coefficients are accounted for by the biproportional adjustment procedure of the RAS. In terms of the aggregate χ^2, the reduction in error after the adjustment is about 43 per cent. This is further confirmed when the two hypotheses are compared in terms of their weighted mean and weighted root mean error sum of squares (i.e. MESS and WRMESS).

The frequency distribution of errors by size of educational coefficients is presented in Table 8.3. This table is further

TABLE 8.2: **Goodness of fit of RAS adjusted occupation-education matrix: Professional and technical workers (public sector—1972)**

Test-statistic	SAB	RAS	RAS/SAB
1. ESS	3.95774	2.27065	.574
2. WESS	.10300	.34708	.457
3. WESS/ESS	.02602	.02073	—
4. WMESS	.00069	.00031	.449
5. WRMESS	.02620	.01761	.672
6. χ^2	549265.6	312989.8	.570

arranged into A and B to represent the negative errors (i.e., error due to over-estimation) and the positive errors (i.e., errors due to the under-estimation), respectively. Both the tables confirm that the smaller coefficients (such as those below 10 per cent of the total employment) are subject to not only more frequent errors but also to higher magnitude of error. With an increase in the size of the coefficients, the frequency of errors declines (see Tables 8.3-A and 8.3-B). In other words, size of the coefficients and frequency of errors are negatively associated. There is thus a possibility of using this technique for arriving at the educational requirements of the professional and technical workers in public sector establishments within an acceptable margin of error.

TABLE 8.3-A: **Distribution of negative errors by size of educational coefficients: Professional and technical workers (public sector—1972)**

Magnitude of errors (%)	Size of educational coefficients (%) 0-10	10-20	20-30	30-40	40-50	50-60	60-70	70-80	80-90	90-100
0-10	1	1	—	—	—	—	—	—	2	1
10-20	3	2	—	—	—	—	2	—	2	—
20-30	3	—	—	—	—	2	—	1	—	—
30-40	1	—	—	1	—	1	—	—	—	—
40-50	4	1	—	—	—	1	3	—	—	—
50-60	3	1	—	—	—	—	—	—	—	—
60-70	—	—	—	—	—	—	—	—	—	—
70-80	—	—	1	—	—	—	—	—	—	—
80-90	1	—	—	1	—	—	—	—	—	—
90-100	—	1	—	—	—	—	—	—	—	—
100 and above	13	1	—	1	—	—	—	—	—	—

TABLE 8.3-B: **Distribution of positive errors of size of educational coefficients: Professional and technical workers (public sector—1972)**

Magnitude of errors (%)	Size of educational coefficients (%)									
	0-10	10-20	20-30	30-40	40-50	50-60	60-70	70-80	80-90	90-100
0-10	1	—	—	—	—	1	1	1	1	—
10-20	2	—	—	—	—	—	2	—	—	—
20-30	2	—	1	—	—	—	—	—	—	—
30-40	—	1	—	1	—	—	—	1	—	—
40-50	3	1	—	—	1	—	—	—	—	—
50-60	5	2	—	—	—	1	—	—	—	—
60-70	6	1	1	—	—	—	—	—	—	—
70-80	10	—	—	—	—	—	—	—	1	—
80-90	6	2	—	—	—	—	—	—	—	—
90-100	30	2	1	—	—	1	—	—	—	—

Mean error = 22.762
Standard deviation = 67.982
Skewness = (—).568
Kurtosis = (—).993

The distribution of errors in terms of the absolute frequencies associated with each error-interval is shown in Figure 8.2. The mean and standard deviation of this distribution are 22.76 and 67.98, respectively (Table 8.3-B). These statistics suggest that (a) the mean error is large, and (b) variations around the mean are considerably large. The fact that the distribution is negatively skewed [coefficients of skewness is (—) 0.568] indicates that there is large negative error in the distribution. The kurtosis, which refers to the peakedness of the distribution in Figure 8.2, works out to be (—) 0.993. It suggests that the distribution is platykurtic and, therefore, has a more flat peak. This may be due to the larger frequencies of educational coefficients associated with higher percentages of errors.

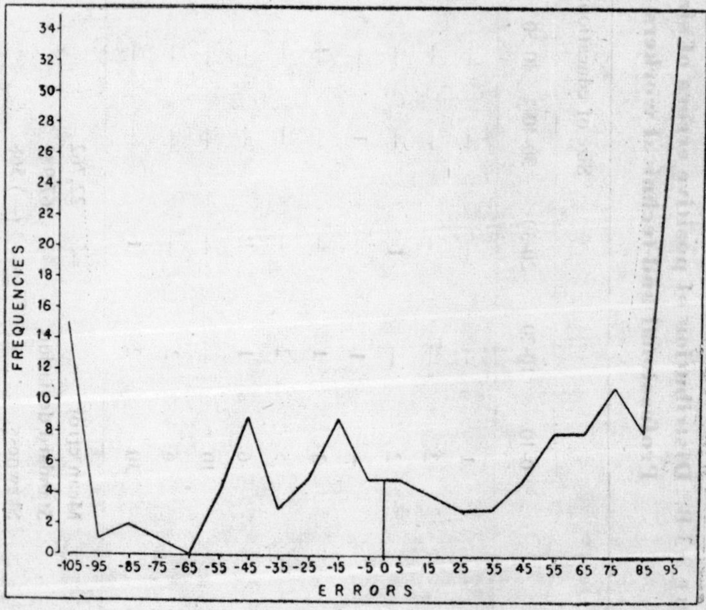

Fig. 8.2: Occupation-education matrix: Professionals (public sector –1972)

Industry-wise analysis of educational profile of workers: Public sector

The exercise reported below relates to four occupational categories of the two public sector manufacturing establishments, viz., the Manufacture of Fertilizers (SIC. 332) and the Manufacture of Machine Tools (SIC. 372). The occupational categories classified at the two digit level include professional and technical workers (Div. 0), managerial and executive workers (Div. 1) and craftsmen and production process workers (Divs. 7 and 8). We first describe the results obtained for the manufacture of fertilizer.

Manufacture of Fertilizer (SIC. 332)

The adjusted occupation-education matrix for 1972 is given in Table 8.4. It can be noticed from this matrix that several coefficients are not plausible. Specifically, the educational coefficients of architects, engineers, biologists (00 and 02) seem doubtful. It can be seen, for example, from Table 8.4 that around 55 per cent of these workers are non-graduates. As against this, the share of those with degrees in Professional Courses turns out to be only 35 per cent and the holders of Degrees in Science are not more than 2 per cent of the total employment in this occupational group. Considering the nature of jobs performed by these workers, a very high share of the 'Below Graduates' cannot be accepted at face value.

The coefficients of 'Below Graduates' attached to Nurses, Pharmacists and Health Technicians (04), Carpenters, Joiners, etc. (77) and Compositors, Printers, etc. (80), are similarly implausible. Table 8.4 shows that almost 100 per cent of the workers in these occupations are 'Below Graduates'. This is again difficult to justify.

The concentration of skill specific education is again revealed by the low values of entropies, shown in Table 8.4. In such occupations as Physicians and Surgeons (03), Nurses and other Health Workers (04), Tailors and Cutters (71), Carpenters, etc. (77), Compositors and Printers (80), etc., the

TABLE 8.4: **RAS adjusted occupation-education coefficient matrix: Manufacture of fertilizer (public sector—1972)**

Occupations / Education	Engineers, Biologists, etc. (00 + 02)	Doctors (03)	Nurses (04)	Teachers (05)	Social Scientists (07)
1. Below Graduates	.5574	.0000	.9655	.2022	.5821
2. Graduate, P.G., Ph. D. in Arts, Commerce and Law etc.	.0006	.0000	.0000	.3103	.2957
3. Graduates, P.G., Ph. D. in Science	.0202	.0001	.0000	.0740	.0129
4. Degree in Professional Courses (including Dip./Cert. in P. Manag. or B. Admns.)	.3467	.9999	.0000	.1444	.0000
5. Dip. in Science and Technology	.0744	.0000	.0312	.1429	.1093
6. Certificate in Trade	.0007	.0000	,0033	.1262	.0000
Adjusted Entropies	.5456	.0005	.0890	.9470	.5431

TABLE 8.4: (*Contd.*)

Education \ Occupations	Draughtsmen, Science and Engineering Technicians (09)	Administrators, Executive Officials (10)	Directors, Managers, etc. (13)	Tailors, Cutters, etc. (71)	Furnacemen, Rollers, Drawers, etc. (73)
1. Below Graduates	.1069	.3880	.1164	.9877	.6158
2. Graduate, P.G., Ph. D. in Arts, Commerce and Law, etc.	.0000	.1786	.0382	.0000	.0000
3. Graduates, P.G., Ph. D in Science	.0000	.0756	.2837	.0000	.0000
4. Degree in Professional Courses (including Dip./Cert. in P. Manag. or B. Admns.)	.2290	.2216	.4984	.0000	.0000
5. Dip. in Science and Technology	.6508	.1265	.0633	.0000	.0000
6. Certificate in Trade	.0133	.0097	.0000	.0123	.3842
Adjusted Entropies	.5092	.8448	.6992	.0362	.3716

TABLE 8.4: (*Contd.*)

Education \ Occupations	Tool makers, Machinists, Plumbers, etc. (75)	Electricians and related Electronic Workers (76)	Carpenters, Joiners, Cabinet makers, etc. (77)	Compositors, Printers, etc. (80)
1. Below Graduates	.2953	.0952	.9999	.9999
2. Graduate, P.G., Ph. D. in Arts, Commerce and Law, etc.	.0000	.0000	.0000	.0000
3. Graduate, P.G., Ph. D. in Science	.0000	.0000	.0000	.0000
4. Degree in Professional Courses (including Dip./Cert. in P. Manag. or B. Admns.)	.0000	.0000	.0000	.0000
5. Dip. in Science and Technology	.2194	.0259	.0000	.0000
6. Certificate in Trade	.4853	.8789	.0001	.0001
Adjusted Entropies	5824	.2409	.0005	.0005

entropies are fairly close to zero. These entropies are .0005, .0890, .0362, .0005 and .0005, respectively.

The values of the test-statistics in Table 8.5 do not favour the SAB hypothesis. Since the test-statistics associated with this hypothesis yield positive values (e.g., ESS=13.000; WESS=0.567; WMESS=0.007; WRMESS=0.082 and χ^2=2378.3), it indicates that occupation-wise educational coefficients do not remain constant during the years for which the results are drawn.

The results of test-statistics associated with the RAS, on the other hand, seem promising. As compared to no adjustment (i.e., SAB), we note from Table 8.5 that the reduction in values of the test-statistics after the RAS adjustment is fairly large. Using the weighted error sum of squares (WESS) as a criterion, we observe that around 85 per cent of the error reduces after the adjustment. The drop in error after the adjustment is also confirmed by WMESS (85.7 per cent) and WRMESS (62 per cent). The reduction in error is, however, only 34 per cent when the aggregate χ^2 is used as a measure of the goodness of fit.

TABLE 8.5: **Goodness of fit of RAS adjusted occupation-education matrix: Manufacture of fertilizer (public sector—1972)**

Test statistic	SAB	RAS	RAS/SAB
1. ESS	13.000	3.216	.247
2. WESS	.567	.083	.146
3. WESS/ESS	.044	.026	—
4. WMESS	.007	.001	.143
5. WRMESS	.082	.031	.378
6. χ^2	2378.3	1559.8	.656

The frequency distribution of negative and positive errors by size of educational coefficients is shown in Tables 8.6-A and 8.6-B, respectively. These tables indicate an inverse relationship between the size of the coefficients and the frequency of the error. It suggests the appropriateness of the RAS method for working out the occupation-education relationships

TABLE 8.6-A: **Distribution of negative errors by size of educational coefficients: Manufacture of fertilizer (public sector—1972)**

Magnitude of errors (%)	Size of educational coefficients (%)									
	0-10	10-20	20-30	30-40	40-50	50-60	60-70	70-80	80-90	90-100
0-10	—	1	1	—	—	—	—	—	—	4
10-20	—	—	—	—	1	—	—	—	—	—
20-30	—	—	—	—	—	1	—	—	—	—
30-40	—	—	1	—	—	—	—	—	—	—
40-50	—	—	—	1	—	—	—	—	—	—
50-60	—	—	—	—	—	—	—	—	—	—
60-70	—	—	—	—	—	—	—	—	—	—
70-80	—	—	—	—	—	—	—	—	—	—
80-90	1	—	—	—	—	—	—	—	—	—
90-100	1	1	—	—	—	—	—	—	—	—
100 and above	8	2	1	—	1	—	—	—	—	—

TABLE 8.6-B: **Distribution of positive errors by size of educational coefficients: Manufacture of fertilizers (public sector—1972)**

Magnitude of errors	Size of educational coefficients (%)									
	0-10	10-20	20-30	30-40	40-50	50-60	60-70	70-80	80-90	90-100
0-10	—	—	—	—	—	—	—	—	—	—
10-20	1	—	—	—	—	—	1	—	—	—
20-30	—	—	—	—	—	—	—	—	—	—
30-40	—	—	1	—	—	—	—	—	—	—
40-50	1	—	—	2	—	1	—	—	—	—
50-60	—	—	—	—	—	—	—	—	1	—
60-70	3	—	—	—	—	—	—	—	—	—
70-80	1	—	1	—	1	—	—	—	—	—
80-90	2	—	1	—	—	2	—	—	—	—
90-100	—	1	1	—	—	—	—	1	—	—

Mean error = (—) 5.425
Standard deviation = 75.229
Skewness = (—) 0.186
Kurtosis = (—) 1.517

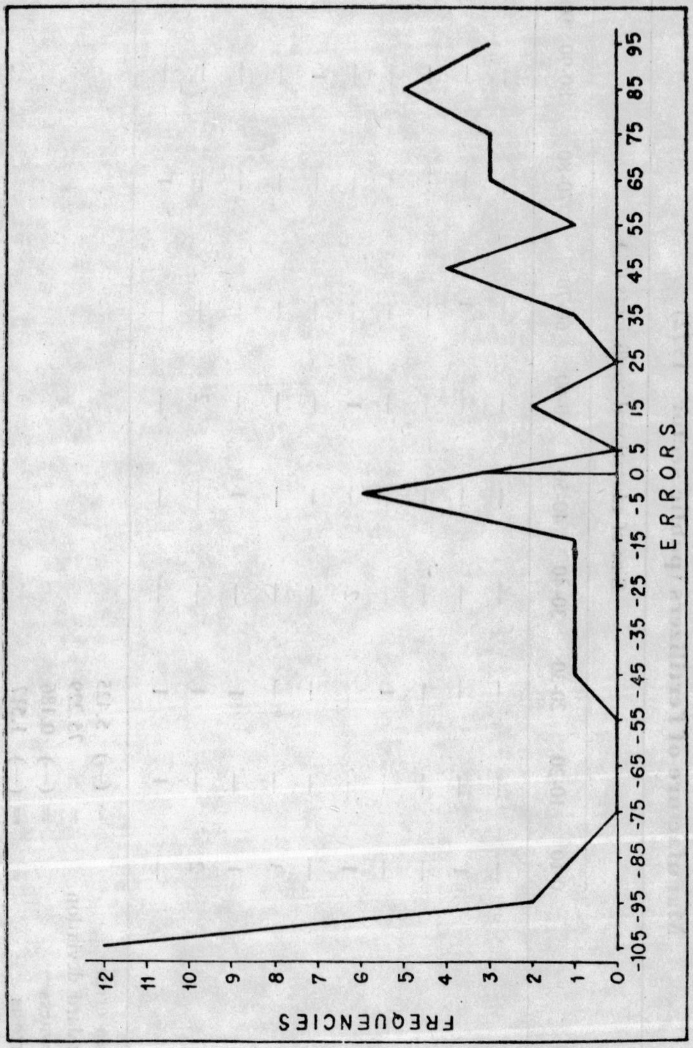

Fig. 8.3: Occupation-education matrix: Manufacture of fertilizer (public sector—1972)

without the risk of a very high margin of error at the aggregate level.

A graphical representation of the distribution of errors (in Tables 8.6 A and 8.6-B is shown in Figure 8.3. Absolute frequencies are represented along the vertical axis while the magnitude of errors on the horizontal axis. The mean and the standard deviation of the underlying distribution turn out to be (—) 5.4 and 75.2, respectively (see Table 8.6-B). There is thus a large variation around the mean error.

Figure 8.3 also suggests that the distribution is negatively skewed [the coefficient of skewness being (—) 0.186] and has a flat peak. The flatness of the peak is confirmed by the value of the kurtosis which is (—) 1.517. The inference, therefore, is that (*a*) the frequency of the negative errors arising out of over-estimation in the adjusted matrix is large, and (*b*) a large number of educational coefficients in the adjusted matrix suffer from high percentages of error.

Manufacture of Machine Tools (SIC. 372)

The adjusted occupation-education coefficients for 1972 are presented in Table 8.7. Here again we encounter implausible coefficients. In particular, the coefficients of Physicians and Surgeons (03) seem implausible as they imply that none of these workers would be professionally qualified. Some other occupational categories which seem to yield implausible coefficients are Nurses and Pharmacists (04), Teachers (05), etc. The coefficients of 'Below Graduate' for these occupations turn out to be as high as 0.533 and 0.767, respectively. Clearly, it is difficult to rely on these coefficients.

That some of the implausible coefficients in the adjusted matrix may have resulted from inaccuracies in the base year, occupation-education matrix cannot be ruled out.

The smaller values of the entropies in Table 8.7, especially in the occupation divisions 7 and 8, reveal concentration of workers within particular educational categories.

The tests for the goodness of fit of the RAS adjusted matrix are reassuring. This is borne out from the values in Table 8.8. Two points may be noted from this table. First, doubts are

TABLE 8.7: **RAS adjusted occupation-education coefficient matrix: Manufacture of machine tools (public sector—1972)**

Occupation / Education	Engineers, Biologists etc. (00+02)	Doctors (03)	Nurses (04)	Teachers (05)	Social Scientists (07)
1. Below Graduate	.0085	.5278	.5328	.7672	.2846
2. Graduate, P.G., Ph.D. in Arts, Commerce and Law etc.	.0016	.0000	.0000	.0000	.7154
3. Graduate, P.G., Ph.D. in Science	.0018	.0000	.0086	.0000	.0000
4. Degree in Professional Courses (including Dip./Cert. in P. Manag. or B. Admns.)	.6093	.0600	.0000	.0000	.0000
5. Dip. in Science and Technology	.3722	.0000	.0746	.2328	.0000
6. Certificate in Trade	.0066	.4122	.3840	.0000	.0000
Adjusted Entropies	.4286	.3913	.5243	.3029	.3335

TABLE 8.7: (*Contd.*)

Education \ Occupation	Draughtsmen, Science and Engineering Technicians (09)	Administrators, Executive officials (10)	Directors, Managers, etc. (13)	Tailors, Cutters, etc. (71)	Furnacemen, Rollers, Drawers, etc. (73)
1. Below Graduate	.4605	.4341	.2559	.9276	.1043
2. Graduate, P.G., Ph.D. in Arts, Commerce and Law etc.	.0000	.0595	.0000	.0000	.0000
3. Graduate, P.G., Ph.D. in Science	.0000	.0048	.0427	.0000	.0000
4. Degree in Professional Courses (including Dip./Cert. in P. Manag. or B. Admns.)	.1204	.0468	.0553	.0000	.3000
5. Dip. in Science and Technology	.4191	.0624	.0466	.0000	.0000
6. Certificate in Trade	.0000	.3924	.5995	.0724	.8957
Adjusted Entropies	.5481	.6914	.6106	.1444	.1862

TABLE 8.7: (*Contd.*)

Occupation / Education	Tool makers, Machinists, Plumbers, etc. (75)	Electricians and related Electronic workers (76)	Carpenters, Joiners, Cabinet makers, etc. (77)	Compositors, Printers, etc. (80)
1. Below Graduate	.3797	.5380	.1668	.0001
2. Graduate, P.G., Ph.D. in Arts, Commerce and Law etc.	.0000	.0000	.0000	.0000
3. Graduate, P.G., Ph.D. in Science	.0014	.0000	.0000	.0000
4. Degree in Professional Courses (including Dip./Cert. in P. Manag. or B. Admns.)	.0000	.0000	.0000	.0000
5. Dip. in Science and Technology	.1257	.0000	.0000	.0000
6. Certificate in Trade	.4932	.4620	.8332	.9999
Adjusted Entropies	.5492	.3852	.2517	.0005

raised about the appropriateness of the SAB hypothesis by non-zero positive values associated with all the test measures (e.g., ESS=32.106; WESS=0.663; WMESS=0.008; WRMESS=0.089; χ^2=3226.9). Second, the RAS provides a better approximation. Making a comparison of the weighted error sum of squares (WESS) of the two, we observe from Table 8.8 that the latter is around 6 per cent of the former. It suggests that around 94 per cent of the error reduces after the biproportional adjustment of the RAS. The weighted mean and weighted root mean error sum of squares (i.e., WMESS and WRMESS) also yield similar results. In terms of the aggregate χ^2, the reduction in error after adjustment is more than 56 per cent (Table 8.8).

TABLE 8.8: **Goodness of fit of RAS adjusted occupation-education matrix: Manufacture of machine tools (public sector—1972)**

Test statistic	SAB	RAS	RAS/SAB
1. ESS	32.106	2.646	.082
2. WESS	.663	.038	.057
3. WESS/ESS	.021	.014	—
4. WMESS	.0079	.0004	.051
5. WRMESS	.089	.021	.236
6. χ^2	3226.9	1407.6	.436

The frequency distributions of negative and positive errors by size of educational coefficients are presented in Tables 8.9-A and 8.9-B, respectively. An inverse relationship between size of educational coefficients and the frequency of errors is suggested. The mean, standard deviation, skewness and kurtosis of this distribution are (−) 9.8, 67.3, (−) 0.101 and (−) 1.3, respectively.

Figure 8.4 provides a graphical representation of this distribution. It can be noticed that the distribution in Figure 8.4 follows closely the distributions represented in Figures 8.2 and 8.3. This is also suggested by the negative coefficients of skewness and kurtosis. There are thus indications that (*a*) the frequency of the negative errors arising out of over-estimation

TABLE 8.9 A: **Distribution of negative errors by size of educational coefficients: Manufacture of machine tools (public sector—1972)**

Magnitude of errors	Size of educational coefficients (%)									
	0-10	10-20	20-30	30-40	40-50	50-60	60-70	70-80	80-90	90-100
0-10	—	—	—	1	—	—	—	—	—	1
10-20	1	—	—	—	—	—	—	—	—	—
20-30	1	—	—	2	—	—	—	—	—	—
30-40	—	—	—	—	1	—	—	—	—	—
40-50	—	—	—	—	1	—	—	—	—	—
50-60	1	—	—	—	—	—	—	—	—	—
60-70	1	—	—	—	—	—	—	—	—	—
70-80	—	—	2	—	—	—	—	—	—	—
80-90	—	—	—	—	—	—	—	—	—	—
90-100	—	1	—	—	—	—	—	—	—	—
100 and above	5	1	2	—	1	—	—	—	—	—

TABLE 8.9-B: **Distribution of positive errors by size of educational coefficients: Manufacture of machine tools (public sector—1972)**

Magnitude of errors	Size of educational coefficients (%)									
	0-10	10-20	20-30	30-40	40-50	50-60	60-70	70-80	80-90	90-100
0-10	—	—	—	—	—	—	—	—	—	1
10-20	1	1	—	—	—	2	1	—	—	1
20-30	1	—	—	—	—	1	—	—	—	—
30-40	—	—	—	—	—	—	1	—	—	—
40-50	—	—	—	—	2	—	—	—	—	—
50-60	—	—	—	—	—	—	—	—	—	—
60-70	2	1	—	—	—	—	—	—	—	—
70-80	—	—	1	—	—	—	—	1	—	—
80-90	1	—	—	1	—	1	—	—	—	—
90-100	—	1	—	—	—	—	1	—	—	—

Mean error = (—) 9.8
Standard deviation = 67.3
Skewness = (—) 0.1
Kurtosis = (—) 1.3

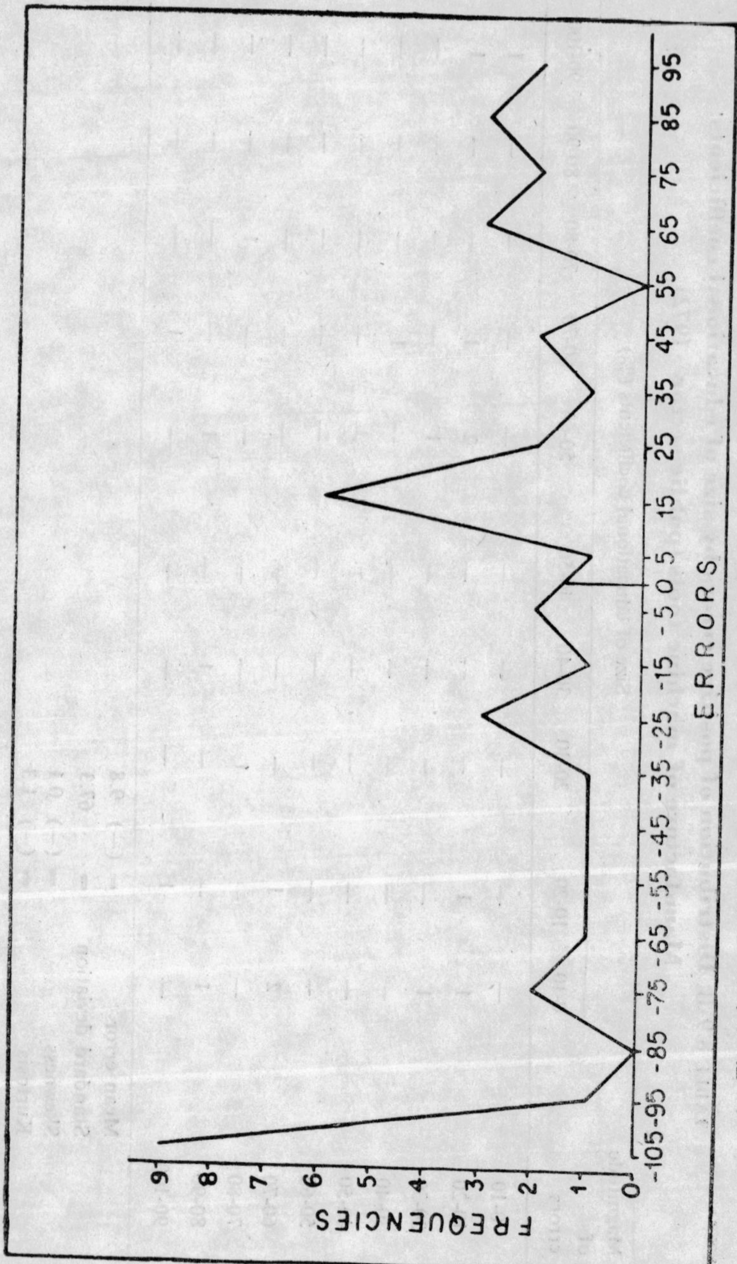

Fig. 8.4: Occupation-education matrix; Manufacture of machine tools (public sector—1972)

in the adjusted matrix is large, and (*b*) many educational coefficients are subject to high percentages of error.

CONCLUDING REMARKS

Based on the data for public sector establishments both after aggregating all such establishments at the all-India level and by industries an attempt was made in this chapter to forecast the occupation-education relationships. Two competing hypotheses have been considered, namely, (*i*) the same as before (SAB), and (*ii*) the RAS adjustment procedure. We summarise below some of the important findings of this exercise.

1. Our results, both after aggregating all the public sector establishments at the all-India level and at the industrial level, favour the RAS adjustment method. The criteria of the goodness of fit in this chapter show that the RAS provides a close approximation to the evolution of the educational coefficients.
2. A measure of the concentration of educational characteristics within occupations, viz., entropy, suggests high degrees of concentration in such occupations as engineers, surgeons, nurses, teachers, tailors and cutters, compositors and printers, etc.
3. We notice that the problem of implausible coefficients is more severe when the adjustments are carried out at the industry level. One possibility may be the inter- or intra-occupational heterogeneity in their occupation-education matrices. (Note that the industry-wise adjustments were carried out for four different occupation divisions.) It is likely that some of the implausible values in the adjusted matrices result from large errors in the base year matrices.
4. The frequency of errors and the size of educational coefficients are inversely related in all the adjusted matrices. The implication is that large cells in the occupation-education matrices are subject to small errors. Hence the use of a RAS adjustment may serve as a basis

for forecasting the occupation-education relationships for short periods of time (i.e , 5-6 years).

REFERENCES

1. A more detailed adjustment procedure incorporating the role of technology and other production characteristics could not be carried out for lack of data. It is important to note that previous studies based on this adjustment have not yielded satisfactory results [see, for example, Layard and Saigal (1966), OECD (1970). Layard *et al* (1971), etc.].
2. For a recent contribution, see Blaug (1970).
3. We will not go into the question whether these abilities are occupation-specific or not.
4. In a few studies, e.g., Bowles (1969), Strimulin (1969), it has been shown that skills can also be acquired through supervised learning on-the-job, work-experience, etc. To illustrate, in some occupations such as Tailors, Cutters and related workers, Furnacemen, Rollers, Drawers, etc., Toolmakers, Mechinists, Plumbers, Welders, etc., the required skills may be acquried either through learning on-the-job or through courses at Industrial Training Institutes. This raises the interesting possibility of alternative methods of skill creation.
5. This has, in fact, been observed by P.R. Panchmukhi, in an unpublished study.
6. Blaug (1970) argues that if homogeneity of job clusters is an important consideration even the U.S. Dictionary of Occupational Titles which distinguishes as many as 20,000 occupations is highly aggregated.
7. The mathematical properties of the equation systems given in equations (8.2) and (8.3) are provided in Bacharach (1970).
8. For a demonstration of this, see Lecomber (1969).
9. For an algebraic formulation of the first four test-statistics, see Chapter 7.

   Note that the aggregate χ^2 test is applied to the corresponding flow matrices. The null-hypothesis for the χ^2 test is that the occupation-education matrices (observed and adjusted) are similar. The algebraic formulations of the aggregate χ^2 for the SAB and the RAS are

$$\sum_{i}\sum_{e} Z^{t}_{ie} \left(\frac{Z^{t+k}}{Z^{t}_{ie}} - 1\right)^{2} \qquad \text{(SAB)}$$

$$\sum_i \sum_e Z_{ie}^{t+k} \left(\frac{\hat{Z}_{ie}^{t+k}}{Z_{ie}^{t+k}} - 1 \right)^2 \qquad \text{(RAS)}$$

10. For a detailed discussion on the concept and computation procedure of entropies, see Chapter 4 (Section 4) of the present study.
11. For a detailed description of the sampling scheme adopted by the DGE&T for the collection of educational qualifications of workers in the private sector, see Appendix 1 of the Occupational-Educational Pattern in India: Private Sector, 1967, Part II.
12. A list of the educational categories used by DGE&T in 1966 and 1972 is provided in Appendix 8.1 of this chapter.
13. Adjusted entropjes are the ratios of actual to maximum entropies, i.e., H/H_{max}. These ratios are used to compare entropies associated with varying number of events. For a detailed discussion, see Chapter 4.

APPENDIX 8.1

CLASSIFICATION OF EDUCATION: 1966 AND 1972

Educational qualification—1966	Education codes	Educational qualification—1972	Education codes
A. **Professional and technical workers**		*A.* **Educational qualification**	
1. Post-graduate (including Ph. D., D. Sc.)	P	1. Below Matric	E
2. Graduate	G	2. Matric and above but below Graduate	F
3. Diploma/Certificate holder	D	3. Graduate	
		(*a*) Science	G
		(*b*) Others (Arts,Co mmerce, Law, etc.)	H
4. With General Educational Qualification but possessing practical experience only		4. Post-graduate including Doctorates	
(*i*) Below Matric	E	(*a*) Arts (including Law)	J
(*ii*) Matriculate but below Graduate	F	(*b*) Science	K

(*iii*) Graduate/Post-graduate		(*c*) Commerce and others	L
(*a*) Arts	H		
(*b*) Science	J		
(*c*) Commerce	K		
(*d*) Others	L		
***B*. Administrative and managerial workers**		***B*. Professional and technical qualification**	
5. Degree/Diploma/Certificate in Personnel Management, Business Administration and similar other qualifications	M	5. Graduate, Post-graduate and Doctorates	
		(*a*) Engineering and Technology	M
		(*b*) Medical	N
		(*c*) Education	P
		(*d*) Agriculture	Q
		(*e*) Business Administration or Personnel Management	R
		(*f*) Others (Chartered Accountant, Social Welfare, etc.)	S
6. Engineering graduate	N	6. Diploma Holders	
7. Engineering diploma holder	Q	(*a*) Engineering and Technology	T
8. Graduate in technology	R	(*b*) Medical	U
9. Diploma holders in technology	S	(*c*) Business Administration or Personnel Management	W
		(*d*) Others	Y

APPENDIX 8.1: (*Contd.*)

10. *With General Educational Qualification*
   - (*i*) Below Matric — E
   - (*ii*) Matriculate but below Graduate — F
   - (*iii*) Graduate/Post-graduate
     - (*a*) Arts — H
     - (*b*) Science — J
     - (*c*) Commerce — K
     - (*d*) Others — L

C. Craftsmen/production process workers

11. Certificate in the Trade from **ITI** or any other Recognised Institution
   - (*i*) Highly skilled — T
   - (*ii*) Skilled — U
   - (*iii*) Semi-skilled — V
12. Practical experience only
   - (*i*) Highly skilled — W
   - (*ii*) Skilled — Y
   - (*iii*) Semi-skilled — Z

7. Graduate and above in Engineering/Technology along with degree, diploma in Business Administration or Personnel Management — D
8. Recognised Certificate Holder — Z
9. Educational Qualification not available — X

APPENDIX 8.2

OCCUPATIONAL TITLES OF PROFESSIONAL AND TECHNICAL WORKERS (NCO 1958)

1	001.00	Civil Engineer
2	002	Mechanical Engineer
3	003	Electrical Engineer
4	006	Mining Engineer
5	001.50	Overseer, Civil and Engineering
6	010	Chemist
7	013	Meteorologist
8	014	Geologist and Geophysicists
9	021.10	Veterinary Surgeon
10	023	Agronomist and Agricultural Scientist
11	020.15	Physician, General
12	030.15	Surgeon, General
13	031.10	Physician, Ayurvedic
14	039.50	Health Officer

APPENDIX 8.2: (Contd.)

15	040.00	Nurse, General
16	041.00	Midwife
17	041.20	Lady Health Visitor
18	050.10	University Teacher, Arts Subjects
19	050.30	University Teacher, Science Subjects
20	050.35	University Teacher, Medicine and Surgery
21	050.45	University Teacher, Agricultural Subjects
22	050.50	University Teacher, Engineer
23	051.10	Secondary School Teacher, General
24	059.10	Secondary School Teacher, Arts (Drawing etc.)
25	059.20	Secondary School Teacher, Manual Craft and Handwork

9

AN OVERALL ASSESSMENT

OBJECTIVE AND SUMMARY OF RESULTS

THE PURPOSE of this study was to investigate inter-temporal changes in the occupational structure of employment and the educational profile of occupation-wise employment in Indian manufacturing industries.

In some important studies—notably by Burgess, Layard and Pant (1968), Ramanujam (1973), etc.—the occupational structure was assumed to remain unchanged over the entire period of projection (see Chapter 2). The detailed occupational data which have become available in recent years cast doubts on the validity of this procedure. In particular, the share of non-manual categories such as professionals and managerial workers has steadily increased in the sixties and seventies (see Table 2.2). Since the non-manual categories are also those which employ the bulk of educated manpower, there is a danger that the assumption of an unchanging occupational structure may result in an underestimation of the educational requirements. These were some of the considerations which have led us to study the changes in the occupational structure of employment.

A review of some features of the data and the adjustments carried out have facilitated an assessment of our results. While constructing the occupation-industry matrices an important consideration was the choice of the occupational classification. Two features of the occupation-industry matrices are: (*a*) a highly skewed distribution of certain skills, and (*b*) the presence of a large number of null cells. One possibility was to use a more aggregated scheme of the occupational classification. However, that might have reduced the information content of the occupation-industry matrices. An attempt was, therefore, made to quantify the loss of information by applying some concepts of information theory. The choice of occupational classification was guided by the consideration that the loss of information should not be more than nominal.

The results of the analysis based on the traditional method of occupational forecasting are presented in Chapter 5. Chapters 6 and 7 give results based on the Markov probability formulation and the RAS adjustment method, respectively. Finally, in Chapter 8 an attempt is made to examine the appropriateness of the RAS adjustment for forecasting the occupation-education relationships. Some of the important findings of these chapters (i.e., from Chapter 5 to Chapter 8) are summarized below.

The traditional method

The traditional method is premised on the assumption that there is a direct and observable relationship between the employment profile and production technology.

Following OECD (1970), the occupational proportions were related to a set of technological and other related factors in the manufacturing sector. In all, 13 occupations and 81 manufacturing establishments were considered. The statistical analysis is based on three cross-sections for 1963-64, 1966-67[1] and 1971-72.

Two formulations were considered. The first formulation is based on the assumption that all the industries in the sample are similar in terms of their production characteristics and lie on the same production function. Alternatively, in the second formulation, intercept and slope differences are explicitly considered by introducing intercept and slope dummies. This was carried out by splitting the sample of industries into five sub-samples, namely, (*i*) the agriculture based industries, (*ii*) the mining and metals based industries, (*iii*) the chemicals based industries, (*iv*) the engineering industries, and (*v*) the miscellaneous industries.

In general, our experiments with the traditional method did not produce very satisfactory results. The temporal variations in the results were large. Specifically, the coefficients of factors which explained inter-industry variations in occupational proportions changed drastically, in some cases, over time. It is, therefore, difficult from these results to determine the factors which are empirically more relevant for forecasting the demand for particular skill(s).

The share of non-production (or non-manual) workers appeared to be more closely associated with the factors representing the production technology—the only exception being managerial workers. In addition to the technological factors, the average output of a firm, used as a proxy for the scale of production, turned out to be an important determinant of most of the skills.

The capital intensity variables and shares of several occupations (e.g., professional and technical workers, clerical workers, workers in transport and communication occupations, etc.) were positively related. This implies that industries with high capital per unit of output are likely to employ more of these skills.

The statistical significance of the intercept and slope dummies confirmed that there are important technological differences between industries in our sample. It may, therefore, be inferred that a straightforward application of the regression analysis assuming that each industry has the same production function might be hazardous for occupational forecasting.

Considering these results, it might be concluded that application of the traditional method to cross-sectional data is unlikely to yield a predictive relationship on the basis of which projections of occupational structure may be attempted.

The Markov probability formulation

An alternative approach to the traditional method is the Markov probability formulation which has often been recommended for forecasting the occupational structure in developing countries on account of its modest data requirements.

This approach can be distinguished from the traditional method in two respects:

(*i*) the focus of the Markov probability approach is on inter-occupational movements as a determinant of temporal changes in the occupational structure of employment; and

(*ii*) this approach explicitly takes into account the inter-dependence between occupational categories (i.e., each occupation influences other occupations and is also influenced by them).

The evolution of the occupational structure in this formulation is viewed as a stochastic process in which inter-occupational movements are governed by a first order Markov system. To estimate the occupational mobility coefficient, a programming model, which minimises the sum of absolute deviations, was used.

This exercise was carried out with the help of time series data on seven years, i.e., 1960-61 to 1972-73 and five occupational categories, namely, professional and technical workers, administrative, executive and managerial workers, clerical and sales workers, production process workers and unskilled workers.

The empirical results, presented in Chapter 6, raised certain doubts about the usefulness of this method for forecasting the structure of employment.

While the approximation to the actual values turned out to be close (the value of the objective function being low in all the exercises that we have carried out), there were two serious difficulties with the results:

(*i*) Some of the transition probabilities (i.e., occuptional mobility coefficients) turned out to be implausible. We note, for example, from Table 6.1 that within a year almost 95 per cent of clerical and sales workers become unskilled workers (P_{35}=0.950).

(*ii*) While the problem of implausible values may be reduced by fixing some of the probabilities in advance, our results suggest that this tends to reduce the predictive power of the model. Moreover, since the probabilities (represented in the form of bounds) are no more than mere guesses, any particular solution is clearly difficult to justify.

The RAS adjustment: Manufacturing sector

Since both the preceding methods of occupational forecasting have failed to yield very satisfactory results, a third method, based on the biproportional adjustment procedure, was applied in Chapter 7. This method consists of adjusting the elements of a base year matrix from the given row and column totals for another year. Its application to occupation-industry matrices for different points of time was attempted to assess its usefulness for short and medium term forecasting. An important feature of this technique is that it required minimal data, viz., an initial occupation-industry matrix, and row and column totals for the year of adjustment.

The tests of this method which have been carried out suggest that the biproportionality rule of the RAS provides a close approximation to the evolution of the occupational structure. The results of these tests also indicate that the underlying biproportionality hypothesis may be more appropriate for short period adjustments.

A significant finding is that the size of the occupational coefficients and the error (after carrying out the RAS adjustment) appear to be inversely related. In other words, the larger the coefficients the lower is the magnitude of error. The errors in the forecasts in absolute terms may, thus, in general, be not large.

Further, the distribution of errors by size of occupational coefficients in the adjusted matrices was negatively skewed (see Figures 7.1, 7.2 and 7.3). This implies large negative errors in the distribution. Since the mean errors for most of the distributions turn out to be negative, it is likely that, in general, the RAS adjustment will tend to overestimate some of the coefficients.

Application of RAS to occupation-education relationships

The manpower forecasting approach to educational planning seeks to link educational expansion to manpower requirements. This requires projection of occupation-education relationships. Considering the simplicity and relatively modest data requirements of the RAS method, experiments were carried out in Chapter 8 to examine its appropriateness for adjusting temporal variations in occupation-education matrices. Our experiments are based on the data for two public sector manufacturing establishments cross-classified by occupational and educational characteristics of workers. A similar experiment at the all India level for professional and technical workers in all the public sector establishments taken together is also attempted.

In general, the results of these experiments favour the RAS adjustment method. The criteria of the goodness of fit show that the RAS provides a close approximation to the evolution of the occupation-education relationships over the period in question.

We notice from these results that the problem of implausible coefficients was more severe when the adjustments were carried out at the industry levels for different occupational groups (viz., professional and technical workers, managerial workers and craftsmen and production process workers). Presumably, some of the implausible values in the adjusted matrices result from large errors in the base year matrices.

The magnitude of errors and the size of educational coefficients were inversely related in all the adjusted matrices. The implication is that large cells in the occupation-education matrices are subject to small errors. Hence, the use of the RAS adjustment may serve as a first approximation for forecasting the occupation-education relationships for short periods of time (i.e., 5-6 years).

CONCLUDING REMARKS

The preceding discussion highlights the merits and some of the limitations of the RAS adjustment of occupation-industry and occupation-education matrices. It is evident from the results that the RAS adjustment provides a close approximation to the evolution of these matrices over a short period of time. When the period of adjustment is extended, the predictive power of the technique in question falls rapidly. Given the data limitations, it is safe to conclude that (*i*) the RAS adjustment is preferable to no adjustment at all; (*ii*) experiments with other techniques of forecasting, which may be intuitively more appealing, but require more detailed data than are currently available, are not likely to produce very reliable results.

Although the RAS emerges relatively unscathed as a method of projecting the occupational/educational structure of employment, some limitations of this method ought not to be overlooked. One of these is the risk that, if the initial value of any particular coefficient is high, it is likely that the adjusted value would be an overestimate. Another limitation is that an exact biproportional hypothesis may be appropriate in only a few specific cases. A third limitation is that while the RAS adjustment helps in reducing the errors in projections, a satisfactory explanation of the factors shaping the occupational structure still eludes us.

An extension of the present study would be to experiment with more flexible versions of the RAS adjustment which allow for random departures from biproportionality. This may reduce the errors in the forecasts. These extensions, however, require more detailed data than the simple RAS adjustment.

REFERENCES

1. The number of establishments in the second cross-section (i.e., 1966-67) was 77.

BIBLIOGRAPHY

Ahmad, B. and Blaug, M. (Ed.) (1973): *The Practice of Manpower Forecasting: A Collection of Case Studies*, Elsevier Scientific Publishing Company, Amsterdam.

Bacharach, M. (1970): *Biproportional Matrices and Input-Output Change*, Cambridge University Press, Cambridge.

Becker, G.S. (1964): *Human Capital: A Theoretical Analysis with Special Reference to Education*, Princeton University Press.

Blaug, M. (1967): "Approaches to Educational Planning", *The Economic Journal*, No. 306, Vol. 77.

Blaug, M. (Ed.) (1968): *Economics of Education*, Penguin Books, London.

Blaug, M. (1970): *An Introduction to Economics of Education*, Penguin Books, London.

Blaug, M. (1976): "The Empirical Status of Human Capital Theory: A Slightly Jaundiced Survey", *Journal of Economic Literature*, Vol. 14, No.3.

Blaug, M., Layard, P.R.G. and Woodhall, M. (1969): *The Causes of Graduate Unemployment in India*, Allen Lane, London.

Bosworth, D.L., Evans, G.J. and Lindley, R.M. (1974): "Mechanistic Manpower Models", in *Problems in Manpower Forecasting*, (Ed.) J. Stuart Wabe, Saxon House Studies, Lexington Books.

Bowles, S. (1969): *Planning Educational System for Economic Growth*, Harvard University Press, Cambridge, Mass.

Burgess, T., Layard, R. and Pant, P. (1968): *Manpower and Educational Development in India, 1961-1986*, Oliver and Boyd, Edinburgh and London.

Dalvi, M.Q. and Prasad, K.N. (1981): "Application of Generalised Inverse and RAS Method to Regionalisation of National Input-Output Tables", *Paper presented to the*

20th Annual Conference of the Indian Econometric Society, New Delhi, 6-8 January, 1982.

Dasgupta, A.K. (1974): *Economic Theory and the Developing Countries*, Macmillan.

Dasgupta, A.K. and Pearce, D.W. (1972): *Cost-Benefit Analysis: Theory and Practice*, Macmillan.

Department of Applied Economics, University of Cambridge (1963): *Input-Output Relationships, 1954-66*, Chapman and Hall, London.

Dougherty, C.R.S. (1972): "Substitution and the Structure of the Labour Force", *The Economic Journal*, Vol. 82, No. 325.

Evans, G.J. and Lindley, R.M. (1972): "The Use of RAS and Related Models in Manpower Forecasting", *Research Paper No. 22*, Centre for Industrial, Economic and Business Research, University of Warwick.

Fields, G.S. (1974): "The Allocation of Resources to Education in Less Developed Countries", *Journal of Public Economics*, Vol. 3, No. 2.

Gaiha, R. (1977): *A Model of Manpower Planning for India*, Unpublished Ph. D. Thesis submitted to the Victoria University of Manchester.

Gaiha, R. (1974): "A Comparative Analysis of Occupational Profiles in Private and Public Sectors in India" (mimeo.), Institute of Economic Growth, Delhi.

Gupta, A.P. (1977): *Fiscal Policy for Employment Generation in India*, Tata McGraw-Hill, New Delhi.

Gupta, A.P. (1983): "Fiscal Policy, Capital Intensity and Employment" in Austin Robinson *et al* (Ed.), *Employment Policy in a Developing Country: A Case Study of India*, Vol. 1, Macmillan, London.

Hansen, W.L. (1963): "Total and Private Rates of Return to Investment in Schooling", *Journal of Political Economy*, Vol. 71, No. 2.

Harberger, A.C. (1965): "Investment in Man Vs. Investment in Machines: The Case of India", in *Education and Economic Development*, (Ed.) M.J. Bowman and C.A. Anderson.

Horowitz, M.A., Zymelman, M. and Harrnstadt, I.L. (1966):

Manpower Requirement for Planning: An International Comparison Approach, North Eastern University.

International Labour Organisation (1971): "Projection of Occupational Structure and Markov Process" in *Investment in Human Resources and Manpower Planning*, New York.

Johansen, L. (1968): "Explorations in Long-Term Projections for the Norwegian Economy", *Economics of Planning*, Vol. 8, No. 1, 2.

Jolly, R. and Colclough, C. (1972): "African Manpower Plans: An Evaluation", *International Labour Review*, Vol. 106, No. 23.

Kadekodi, G. and Gaiha, R. (1976): "Dynamics of Occupational Structure: A Comparative Analysis of U.S.A., Japan, and India", *Paper presented at the Third World Econometric Congress in Toronto.*

Kmenta, J. (1971): *Elements of Econometrics*, Macmillan.

Krishnan, P. (1974): Occupational Mobility in India, 1961-1971", *Paper presented to the Third Data Base Seminar on Indian Economy*, New Delhi, December 29-31.

Layard, P.R.G. (1972): "Economic Theories of Educational Planning", in *Essays in Honour of Lord Robbins*, (Ed.) M. Preston and B. Corry, Weidenfeld and Nicolson.

Layard, P.R.G. and Saigal, J.C. (1966): "Educational and Occupational Characteristics of Manpower: An International Comparison", *British Journal of Industrial Relations*, Vol. 4, No. 2.

Layard, P.R.G., Sargan, J.D., Ager, M.E. and Jones, D.J. (1971): *Qualified Manpower and Economic Performance: An Inter-Plant Study in the Electrical Engineering Industry*, Allen Lane, The Penguin Press, London.

Lecomber, R. (1969): "RAS Projections When Two or More Complete Matrices are Known", *Economics of Planning*, Vol. 9, No. 3.

Lee, T.C., Judge, G.G. and Takayama, T. (1965): "On Estimating the Transition Probabilities of a Markov Process", *Journal of Farm Economics*, Vol. 47, No. 3.

Lee, T.C., Judge, G.G. and Zellner, A. (1970): *Estimating the Parameters of the Markov Probability Model from Aggregate*

Time Series Data, North-Holland Publishing Company, Amsterdam.

Merrett, S. (1966): "The Rate of Return to Education—A Critique", *Oxford Economic Papers*, Vol. 18, No. 3.

Nallagounden, A.M. (1967): "Investment in Education in India", *Journal of Human Resources*, Vol. 2, No. 3.

Organisation for European Co-operation and Development (OECD) (1970): *Occupational and Educational Structures of the Labour Force and Levels of Economic Development: Possibilities and Limitations of an International Comparison Approach*, Paris.

Organisation for European Co-operation and Development (OECD) (1971): *Occupational and Educational Structures of the Labour Force and Levels of Economic Development (Further Analyses and Statistical Data)*, Paris.

Pandit, H.N. (Ed.) (1969): *Measurement of Cost, Productivity and Efficiency of Education*, NCERT, New Delhi.

Parikh, A. (1979): "Forecasts of Input-Output Matrices Using the RAS Method", *The Review of Economic and Statistics*, Vol. 61, No. 3.

Parnes, H. (1962): *Forecasting Educational Needs for Economic and Social Development*, OECD, Paris.

Ramanujam, M.S. (1973): "Requirements of Technical Manpower in India: 1965-66 to 1980-81", *Indian Economic Review*, Vol. 8, No. 2.

Sabolo, Y. (1971): "A Structural Approach to the Projection of Occupational Categories and Its Application to S. Korea and Taiwan", *International Labour Review*, Vol. 103, No. 2.

Schultz, T.W. (1963): *The Economic Value of Education*, Columbia University Press, New York and London.

Sen, A.K. (1966): "Economic Approaches to Education and Manpower Planning", *The Indian Economic Review*, Vol. 1 (New Series), No. 1.

Shrinivasan, K.N. and Raj, D. (1977): "Comparability of Data on 'Workers' in the 1961 and 1971 Censuses", in *Population Statistics in India* (*Data Base of Indian Economy*, (Ed.) Ashish Bose *et al*, Vol. III, Vikas Publishing House, New Delhi.

Sinha, J.N. (1972): "A Rational View of Census Economic Data", *Indian Journal of Industrial Relations*, Vol. 8, No. 2.

Sinha, J.N. and Sawhney, P.K. (1970): *Wages and Productivity in Selected Indian Industries*, Vikas Publications, Delhi.

Strumilin, S.G. (1969): "The Economic Significance of National Education", in *Economics of Education*, (Ed.) E.A.G. Robinson, and J.E. Vaizey, Macmillan.

Tinbergen, J. and Bos, H.C. (1964): "A Planning Model of Education Requirements of Economic Development", in *The Residual Factor and Economic Growth*, OECD.

Tinbergen, J. and Correa, H. (1962): "Qualitative Adaptation of Education to Accelarated Growth", *Kyklos*, Vol. 15.

Telser, L.G. (1963): "Least Squares Estimation of Transition Probabilities", in *Measurement in Economics*, (Ed.) C.F. Christ, Stanford University Press.

Theil, H. (1967): *Economics and Information Theory*, North-Holland Publishing Company, Amsterdam.

Theil, H. (1972): *Statistical Decomposition Analysis*, North-Holland Publishing Company, Amsterdam.

Government of India reports

Central Statistical Organisation, Department of Statistics (1963, 1966, 1971): *Annual Survey of Industries*, Vol. 1.

Directorate General of Employment and Training (D.G.E. & T.), Ministry of Labour, Employment and Rehabilitation (1960, 1962, 1964): *Reports on Occupational Pattern in India—Public Sector*.

D.G.E. & T. (1966, 1968, 1970, 1972): *Reports on Occupational-Educational Pattern in India—Public Sector.*

D.G.E. & T. (1961, 1963, 1965): *Reports on Occupational Pattern in India—Private Sector.*

D.G.E. & T. (1967, 1969, 1971, 1973): *Reports on Occupational-Educational Pattern in India—Private Sector.*

D.G.E. & T. (1967): *Occupational-Educational Pattern in India—Private Sector*, Part II.

Ministry of Education (1970): *Report of the Education Commission (1964-1966).*

National Sample Survey: *Report on the Survey of Employment and Unemployment*, 32nd Round, July 1977-June 1978, Number 298.

Perspective Planning Division, Planning Commission: *Notes on a Perspective of Development in India, 1960-61 to 1975-76.*

Registrar General and Census Commissioner of India, Census of India (1971): *Report on Resurvey on Economic Questions—Some Results*, Miscellaneous Studies, Paper 1, 1974.

Registrar General and Census Commissioner of India, Census of India (1971): Degree Holders and Technical Personnel (Special Tables G-V—G-XII), Series 1, India.

INDEX